How Many Judges

Does It Take to Make

a Supreme Court?

How Many Judges Does It Take to Make a Supreme Court?

And Other Essays on Law

and the Constitution

John V. Orth

University Press of Kansas

Published by the University Press of Kansas (Lawrence, Kansas 66045), which
was organized by the Kansas Board of Regents and is operated and funded by
Emporia State University, Fort Hays State University, Kansas State University,
Pittsburg State University, the University of Kansas, and Wichita State University

Library of Congress Cataloging-in-Publication Data

Orth, John V.

How many judges does it take to make a Supreme Court? : and other
essays on law and the constitution / John V. Orth.

p.   cm.

Includes bibliographical references and index.

ISBN 978-0-7006-1478-3 (cloth : alk. paper)

ISBN 978-0-7006-1479-0 (pbk. :alk. paper)

1. Judicial power—United States. 2. Common law—United States. I. Title.

KF5130 .O78 2006

347.73'12—dc22   2006013564

British Library Cataloguing-in-Publication Data is available.

Printed in the United States of America

10 9 8 7 6 5 4 3 2 1

Contents

Preface

L aw schools do some things very well, like teaching students the skills of legal reasoning, "how to think like a lawyer." Of course, everyone knows that more than mental acuity is required to make a good, let alone a great, lawyer. That requires, in addition to reasoning ability, many other things such as rhetorical skills, strategic sense, ethical sensitivity, and qualities of humanity, common sense, and imagination, not to mention knowledge of fields other than law, like politics and economics—which is why some students who do very well in law school do not do so well in the practice of law (and vice versa). But because legal education is so focused on teaching legal reasoning, there are some topics, even topics that could be taught in the classroom but that do not fit comfortably within current curricular categories, that evade systematic study in law school. This collection of essays is an attempt to explore some of these neglected but important topics.

Law students typically learn their law from the study of reports of judicial opinions, which is why in law schools the "casebook" takes the place of the textbook normally found in higher education. But while appellate cases and the judges who decide them are at the center of legal education, no attention is usually paid to the question in the title of the first essay, *"How many judges does it take to make a supreme court?"* The answer, as it turns out, is not trivial in the history of law and the constitution. Once judges secured protection from removal except for misbehavior, and then only by the cumbersome means of impeachment, politicians who wanted to influence the course of judicial decision sometimes invoked their power to alter the number of judges. In the course of charting the changing size of the Supreme Court, a surprising fact emerges: that what seems obvious today—that however many judges there are on an appellate court, there must always be an odd number—was not always so obvious. For most of the long history of the common law, as well as for the first years of the U.S. Supreme Court, there was an even number of judges. The felt need for an odd number, so that a "tiebreaker" would always be available, suggests a changed perception of law, at least at the level of a court of last resort, a perception that law, like electoral politics, is a matter of votes, not a matter of fact on which well-trained jurists would most often agree.

Law school casebooks are, as their name implies, made up of reports of decided cases, yet no systematic attention is paid in law school to the production of these reports. They are simply assumed to be accurate accounts of what went on in court and in many cases of what went on in the world outside the courtroom. There is a good reason for that: ever since the foundation of the modern law school in the late nineteenth century, the accuracy of the reports could be taken for granted. But a look at the history of law reporting over the centuries shows that accurate and available reports are, as they are called in the second essay, one of *"the secret sources of judicial power."* As belief in the obviousness and accessibility of law waned, the opinions of the judges on exactly what the law was grew in importance. And because our legal system, derived from English common law, was based on precedent, the more that was known about what the judges decided (and why), the more powerful they became. Closely related to this is the recognition of another little-noticed source of judicial power: the unitary "opinion of the court," a uniquely American practice, unknown in other countries that trace their legal tradition to England. And the institutional position of the courts, their control over legal procedure, for example, lends them more power in some situations than in others, leverage that great judges astutely employ.

Nowhere in the law school curriculum except perhaps in a course on legal history, and even then only in a course not devoted solely to the history of American law, does the student consider the remarkable longevity of the common law. It is generally accepted that the common law originated more than 800 years ago in England. Yet this medieval relic from across the sea still serves as the basic organizing principle of modern American law. The antiquity of the common law means that it long predated written constitutions, another American legal innovation. The interaction of the common law and the constitution is the subject of the next essay. Laws can be unconstitutional, especially when they are cast in the form of statutes, but *"can the common law can be unconstitutional?"* In theory, the answer must also be yes, but the story in this case is more complicated. Not only is the common law not comprehensively set forth in a written text, but the same judges who determine what it is also interpret the constitution, rendering the chances for conflict between the two less likely. Yet the common-law tradition of strong judges making (and sometimes unmaking) the common law fits uneasily within the structure of a government of separated powers in which the legislative power is vested in elected representatives, and it sometimes appears that rules of the common law can be changed in ways that would be unconstitutional if done by legislation.

Not only is the common law far older than any written constitution; it is also older than all statutes. Although statutes have been known almost (but not quite) since the beginning of the common law 800 years ago, they became a predominant part of the common-law system only in the last century or two. Until the nineteenth century, legislation played only a small part in private law other than property law. This alone is worth remarking, since most people, including most beginning law students, assume that a "law" is typically a statute—the source of the old joke about a friendly relative asking a law student how many laws he learned today. The historical priority of the common law over statutes (and written constitutions) means that the newcomers interact, sometimes in unexpected ways, with the existing law and legal tradition. Some of the consequences are explored in the essay on *"the persistence of the common law."*

Nowadays law, like everything else, is often discussed in terms of ideology. "Liberal" and "conservative" labels are pinned on judges, and classrooms of constitutional law can become arenas of political controversy. Even as to private law topics, claims have been made about the values incorporated in the common law. In and of itself, it is hardly surprising that law expresses values, since it has always been intimately connected with morality, politics, and economics. But when it is specified that private law incorporates values of individualism and economic efficiency, recognition of the antiquity of the common law inspires another inquiry: If the common law is a product of the Middle Ages, how did it come to express such essentially modern values? In fact, for most of its long history the common law was preoccupied with procedure and property, and it is in those two areas that the core values of the common law are to be found. The next essay explores *"the ideology of the common law."*

Last, as is appropriate for the final essay in this collection, is an investigation of how the common law uses what it learns about the past, *"looking backward, looking forward."* Cases, as has been noted, are at the center of law and legal education in the common-law world, and cases begin with inquiries into what happened in the past, a species of historical research. Yet on closer examination it appears that the historical inquiry conducted at a trial is of a very limited kind, constrained by restrictive rules of evidence and tightly focused on one or a very few specific questions. A trial is really concerned about the past only as it bears on what to do in the future, at the conclusion of the trial—and beyond, in the next similar case. This shapes the way legal inquiries are conducted and should shape the way legal rules are constructed. Backward glances, such as are attempted in these essays, may also provide clues about where our legal system is headed, not in the sense of the old, clichéd "lessons of history," but in the sense of insight into the dynamics that drive the system. Looking forward, of course, involves recognition that the common law is constantly in motion, using and reusing the techniques that kept it viable for so long.

That I have answered all the questions I have asked is more than I could hope for. That I have stimulated others to add their information and insights to extend the inquiry is my goal, as it is the goal of all true education whether in law or anything else.

Acknowledgments

Two of the six essays in this collection appeared earlier in somewhat different form: "How Many Judges Does It Take to Make a Supreme Court?" in 19 *Constitutional Commentary* 681–692 (2002), and "The Secret Sources of Judicial Power" in 50 *Loyola Law Review* 529–547 (2004).

A Note on Notes

This book is written to be read "above the line," that is, above the line separating footnotes and text. The notes' principal function is to provide citations to the sources of quotations, to the official reports of cases and compilations of statutes mentioned in the text, and to sources both secondary and primary supportive of assertions in the text. In a few cases the notes include further comments qualifying or amplifying the text, but these are intended only for those with an interest in pursuing (or contesting) the points to which they refer. My views are fully expressed in the text alone, and anyone interested in them may simply ignore the notes.

How Many Judges

Does It Take to Make

a Supreme Court?

I

How Many Judges Does It Take to Make a Supreme Court?

How many judges does it take to make a supreme court? Three? Five? Seven? Nine? Or more? If state as well as federal courts are considered, all answers have been correct at one time or another, in one court or another. State constitutions sometimes set the number of judges; sometimes, like the U.S. Constitution, they leave it to the legislature to decide.[1] The size of a court is usually determined by more or less objective considerations, such as the cost of the

---

1. U.S. CONST. art. III, § 1 (not determining number of supreme court justices). The North Carolina Supreme Court has consisted at various times of three, five, and seven judges. Although the North Carolina Constitution empowers the legislature to increase the size to nine, N.C. CONST. art. IV, § 6, the number remains today at seven. *See* JOHN V. ORTH, THE NORTH CAROLINA STATE CONSTITUTION: A REFERENCE GUIDE 106 (1993).

judicial establishment, the size of the caseload, or the existence of other judicial duties such as circuit-riding, but occasionally—in notorious cases—the number of judges is increased or decreased to serve partisan purposes. "We are under a Constitution," Charles Evans Hughes, a future chief justice, once remarked off-the-cuff and to his everlasting regret, "but the Constitution is what the judges say it is."[2] As the politicians are well aware, sometimes it matters not just who the judges are but how many.[3]

Ever since the Judiciary Act of 1869,[4] the authorized strength of the U.S. Supreme Court has remained at nine. So long accustomed to that number have we become that it seems just about perfect—not too large, not too small. State supreme courts tend not to exceed the federal number. With larger caseloads but smaller jurisdictional areas, they typically function today with nine, seven, or five judges.

Although the size of the U.S. Supreme Court has remained constant since 1869, the status quo was memorably challenged in 1937, when President Franklin Roosevelt proposed his Court Reform Bill, better known to history as the "court-packing plan," designed to secure a majority of jus-

---

2. THE AUTOBIOGRAPHICAL NOTES OF CHARLES EVANS HUGHES 143 (David J. Danelski & Joseph S. Tulchin eds. 1973). Hughes always insisted that his much-quoted comment was misunderstood. *Id.* at 143–144.

3. *See* 1 JAMES BRYCE, AMERICAN COMMONWEALTH 276 (new ed. 1913) (describing legislative control over the number of judges as "a joint in the court's armour through which a weapon might some day penetrate").

4. Act of April 10, 1869, ch. 22, 16 Stat. 44.

tices to uphold the government's economic program.[5] Authorizing the president to appoint one new justice for every sitting justice over the age of seventy, the bill provided for a maximum complement of as many as fifteen judges. Never adopted, the proposal foundered on a public consensus that it would have too obviously politicized the judicial branch. In any event, a majority of the sitting justices rather suddenly coalesced in support of the president's program, the so-called switch in time that saved nine.[6]

For the first century of American history, the number of U.S. Supreme Court justices was closely tied to the number of federal judicial circuits. The connection was forged by the original Judiciary Act in 1789, which created the federal judicial system of district and circuit courts, topped by a supreme court. Although the act provided for the appointment of district court judges and supreme court justices, no circuit

5. *See* William E. Leuchtenburg, *The Origins of Franklin D. Roosevelt's "Courtpacking" Plan, in* William E. Leuchtenburg, The Supreme Court Reborn: The Constitutional Revolution in the Age of Roosevelt 82 (1995); *id.* at 132.

6. The provenance of this phrase is discussed in Michael Ariens, *A Thrice-Told Tale, or Felix the Cat,* 107 Harv. L. Rev. 620, 623 n. 11 (1994). Whether the "switch" was in response to the court-packing plan has been the subject of debate. *See* Richard D. Friedman, *A Reaffirmation: The Authenticity of the Roberts Memorandum, or Felix the NonForger,* 142 U. Pa. L. Rev. 1985 (1994). *See also* William Lasser, *Justice Roberts and the Constitutional Revolution of 1937—Was There a "Switch in Time"?* 78 Tex. L. Rev. 1347 (2000) (reviewing Barry Cushman, Rethinking the New Deal Court: The Structure of a Constitutional Revolution).

judgeships were authorized. Instead, the circuit courts were to be staffed by judges from the other two courts. At first, the nation was divided into three judicial circuits, each to be visited twice yearly by two supreme court justices, who in combination with the resident district court judge would form the circuit court.[7] Although compatible with the federal organization of the new United States, the circuit system was probably inspired by the English system of assize courts, staffed by judges sent out from the central courts. The number of circuits inevitably grew with the nation, but political considerations often played a role in determining when to recognize new circuits and which states to include. The assignment of the states in the circuits was important because of the tradition of placing one representative from each circuit on the court.

Circuit riding quickly became an object of complaint with the justices. Particularly onerous in the early days, it was never easy for the elderly men typically appointed to the court. Justice James Iredell of North Carolina, who drew the Southern Circuit in the 1790s, was described as leading "the life of a post boy," traveling as much as 1,900 miles in a single circuit.[8] Even as transportation improved to make travel less

---

7. Act of Sept. 24, 1789, ch. 20, 1 Stat. 73, § 4. See Wythe Holt, *"To Establish Justice": Politics, the Judiciary Act of 1789, and the Invention of the Federal Courts,* 1989 DUKE L. J. 1421; WILFRED J. RITZ, REWRITING THE HISTORY OF THE JUDICIARY ACT OF 1789: EXPOSING MYTHS, CHALLENGING PREMISES, AND USING NEW EVIDENCE (1990).

8. WILLIS WHICHARD, JUSTICE JAMES IREDELL 173 (2000).

difficult, the nation expanded in size to make the distances to be covered ever greater. In 1793 it was provided that only one supreme court justice was required to visit each circuit.[9] In 1801, as we will see, circuit riding was briefly eliminated but was quickly restored the next year, under circumstances that made further changes difficult. Although the circuits were periodically reconstituted over the years, the number of justices seemed for long inescapably tied to the number of circuits.

At last, the process of breaking the link began when circuit judgeships were finally authorized by the Judiciary Act of 1869, the same act that stabilized the Court's membership at nine.[10] Nominal circuit-riding duties for the justices continued—one supreme court justice was still expected to visit each circuit once in two years—until the creation in 1891 of the circuit courts of appeals (since 1948 called simply the courts of appeals).[11] Today, the remaining circuit duties of the justices are merely vestigial. Applications for stays, for bail, or for extensions of time are addressed to the circuit justice for the circuit in which the case arises.[12] Now that there are

9. Act of March 2, 1793, ch. 22, 1 Stat. 333.

10. Act of April 10, 1869, ch. 22, 16 Stat. 44.

11. Act of March 3, 1891, ch. 517, 26 Stat. 826 (Evarts Act). The circuit courts as such (as opposed to the circuit courts of appeals) continued in existence until 1911, when their jurisdiction was transferred to the district courts. Act of March 3, 1911, ch. 231, 36 Stat. 1087 (Judicial Code).

12. Supreme Court Rule 22.

fourteen circuits, some justices must necessarily be assigned to more than one circuit.[13]

Nine as the designated number of circuits and justices was first attained in 1837. Although proposals to increase the number of circuits and justices had been heard for years, legislation had always foundered on concern about giving the extra appointments to the incumbent president. Finally, on March 3, 1837, the last day of President Andrew Jackson's last term, a new judiciary act was signed into law.[14] Nine was to be the final answer to the question concerning the size of the U.S. Supreme Court, but the upheaval of the Civil War caused a couple of temporary variations. In 1863 Congress increased the size of the Court from nine to ten, in order to provide a circuit justice for an additional circuit created on the admission of California,[15] and to permit President Abraham Lincoln to name the Democratic but Unionist Stephen J. Field to the court.

In 1866 a short-lived judiciary act reduced the number of justices from ten to seven after three vacancies to deny President Andrew Johnson any judicial appointments. The origi-

13. For the current assignments, see the front matter in the U.S. Reports.

14. Act of March 3, 1837, ch. 34, 5 Stat. 176. *See* 2 CHARLES WARREN, THE SUPREME COURT IN UNITED STATES HISTORY 313–314 (1922).

15. Act of March 3, 1863, ch. 100, 12 Stat. 794. *See* CHARLES FAIRMAN, RECONSTRUCTION AND REUNION, 1864–88, PART ONE 2 (1971), vol. 6 of OLIVER WENDELL HOLMES DEVISE HISTORY OF THE SUPREME COURT OF THE UNITED STATES.

nal proposal was to revert to nine justices, "thereby creating an odd number of justices and making the Court more manageable," but the number was reduced for political purposes. In fact, the size of the Court did not drop below eight before the 1869 Judiciary Act, adopted after President Johnson had left office, returned the authorized strength to nine.[16] The extra appointment was helpful to the incoming president Ulysses Grant in securing reversal of the first Legal Tender Case.[17]

The Court's membership had reached seven in 1807.[18] Before that, throughout the first two decades of the Court's existence, the authorized number of justices had generally held at six. The Judiciary Act of 1789 had set the pattern: "The supreme court of the United States shall consist of a chief justice and five associate justices...."[19] In a notorious maneuver in 1801 the Federalist Party, having lost the election of 1800, used its lame-duck majority to pass a new judiciary act that combined many admirable features, including the elimination of circuit riding and the creation of circuit courts

16. Act of April 10, 1869, ch. 22, 16 Stat. 44. *See* 3 WARREN, *supra* note 14, at 144, 223; OXFORD COMPANION TO THE SUPREME COURT OF THE UNITED STATES 475 (Kermit L. Hall ed. 1992).

17. *Hepburn v. Griswold*, 75 U.S. (8 Wall.) 603 (1870), *rev'd by Knox v. Lee*, 79 U.S. (12 Wall.) 457 (1871). *See* OXFORD COMPANION TO THE SUPREME COURT OF THE UNITED STATES, *supra* note 16, at 498–499.

18. Act of Feb. 24, 1806, ch. 16, 2 Stat. 420.

19. Act of Sept. 24, 1789, ch. 20, 1 Stat. 73, § 1.

of appeals, with a reduction in the size of the Court from six to five on the next vacancy—apparently to deny the incoming president, Thomas Jefferson, the opportunity to make an appointment.[20] The victorious Jeffersonians, of course, lost no time in using their newfound legislative power to reverse the Federalist measure. A repeal act, adopted March 8, 1802, the first act of the new Congress, restored the status quo ante, jettisoning the good with the bad and returning the authorized strength of the Court to six.[21] Yet another judiciary act canceled the 1802 term of the court,[22] apparently to delay the hearing of *Marbury v. Madison*, a case with implications for the constitutionality of the abolition of the courts of appeals.[23]

Legislative fiddling with the number of judges was perhaps a necessary consequence of the judiciary's newfound security of tenure. *Durante bene placito*, "during good pleasure," were the Latin words that originally described a common-law judge's term of office, as they still describe the term of the lord chancellor, titular head of the English judiciary.[24]

20. Act of Feb. 13, 1801, ch. 4, 2 Stat. 89. *See* Katherine Turner, *Federalist Policy and the Judiciary Act of 1801*, 22 WILL. & MARY Q. 3 (1965).

21. Act of March 8, 1802, ch. 8, 2 Stat. 132.

22. Act of April 29, 1802, ch. 31, 2 Stat. 156.

23. 5 U.S. (1 Cranch) 137 (1803). *See* JOHN V. ORTH, THE JUDICIAL POWER OF THE UNITED STATES: THE ELEVENTH AMENDMENT IN AMERICAN HISTORY 31–34 (1987).

24. DAVID M. WALKER, THE OXFORD COMPANION TO LAW 384 (1980).

Quamdiu se bene gesserit, "so long as he shall behave himself well," was the formula adopted in England after the Act of Settlement in 1701 to indicate that a judge could be removed only for good cause shown.[25]

Good behavior tenure was not granted to colonial judges by the act, and its denial was one of the grievances of the rebellious colonies. A Philadelphia lawyer too candidly reminded a royal appointee that holding office at pleasure was "a disagreeable tenure to any officer, but a dangerous one in the case of a judge."[26] The Declaration of Independence duly included in its bill of particulars against King George III: "He has made judges dependent on his will alone, for the tenure of their offices, and the amount and payment of their salaries." The U.S. Constitution in 1787, dispensing with Latinity, provided that federal judges hold their offices "during good Behaviour."[27] Although the Jeffersonians early

25. 12 & 13 Will. 3, c. 2, § 3 (1701). For the later history of judicial tenure in England, see David Lemmings, *The Independence of the Judiciary in the Eighteenth Century, in* THE LIFE OF THE LAW: PROCEEDINGS OF THE TENTH BRITISH LEGAL HISTORY CONFERENCE (Peter Birks ed. 1993), and—for the years after 1880—ROBERT STEVENS, THE INDEPENDENCE OF THE JUDICIARY: THE VIEW FROM THE LORD CHANCELLOR'S OFFICE (1993).

26. JAMES ALEXANDER, A BRIEF NARRATIVE OF THE CASE AND TRIAL OF JOHN PETER ZENGER 84 (Stanley Nider Katz ed. 1963) (argument of Hamilton, attorney for defendant). Hamilton, from Philadelphia, volunteered his services for the defense; his client's subsequent acquittal made "Philadelphia lawyer" proverbial. *See* JOHN CIARDI, A BROWSER'S DICTIONARY 298 (1980).

27. U.S. CONST. art. III, § 1. *See generally* John V. Orth, *Who Judges the Judges?* 32 FLA. ST. U. L. REV. 1245 (2005).

experimented with impeachment as a means of cleansing the federal bench of their enemies, the obvious partisanship of the trial of Justice Samuel Chase in 1804 made that method of judicial discipline costly and unreliable.[28]

Without a ready means of removing a judge, the obvious legislative alternative was heightened scrutiny during the confirmation process—and playing the numbers game by increasing (or decreasing) the size of the court. The political object might be to affect the course of judicial decision, as with the 1937 court-packing plan, or simply to increase (or decrease) the number of appointments available to a certain president, as with the 1863 act shrinking the Supreme Court during President Andrew Johnson's term of office. Alternatively, Congress could try to fiddle with the Court's jurisdiction under the "exceptions and regulations" clause of the federal Constitution.[29]

How many judges does it take to make a supreme court? Three? Five? Seven? Nine? Fifteen? All the most frequently given answers have one obvious thing in common: they are

28. STEPHEN B. PRESSER, THE ORIGINAL MISUNDERSTANDING: THE ENGLISH, THE AMERICANS AND THE DIALECTIC OF FEDERALIST JURISPRUDENCE 156–158 (1991).

29. U.S. CONST. art. III, § 2 ("In all the other Cases beforementioned, the supreme Court shall have appellate Jurisdiction, both as to Law and Fact, with such Exceptions, and under such Regulations as the Congress shall make.").

all odd numbers. The restriction of the range of likely answers to odd numbers, of course, makes perfect sense: if the
court is fully staffed and all judges participate, the possibility
of a tie vote is eliminated.[30] The drafters of the first judiciary
act presumably overlooked the necessity to provide a casting
vote in case of a tie when they authorized a supreme court of
six, bemused by the need to correlate the number of justices
with the number of circuits. The founding generation was
certainly not unaware of the possibility of disagreement in
other government departments. The vice president was given
a vote in the Senate if "they be equally divided."[31] The drafters of the 1802 act, which restored the Court's authorized
strength to six from five, were apparently intent only on un-
doing the work of their political enemies. The choice of the
anomalous ten justices, briefly authorized during the Civil
War, was necessitated by pressing political concerns and was
promptly abandoned with the passing of the necessity. The
only question at the time was whether to revert to nine or
seven.

If an odd number of judges is so obviously desirable,
it is curious (one is tempted to say odd) that the premier

30. In case of vacancy, absence, or recusal, an evenly divided appellate
court leaves the lower court's decision in effect. For a defense of current
practice, see Edward A. Hartnett, *Ties in the Supreme Court of the United
States*, 44 WM. & MARY L. REV. 643 (2002). What would happen in the
event of an evenly divided court in a case within the Supreme Court's
original jurisdiction is unknown.

31. U.S. CONST. art. I, § 3.

common-law courts, the Court of King's Bench, the Court of Common Pleas, and the Court of Exchequer, operated for so many centuries with four judges each.[32] In a striking simile, Francis Bacon likened the "twelve Judges of the realm" to the "twelve lions under Solomon's Throne" mentioned in the Bible.[33] Of course, these courts were not "supreme" in the sense of the U.S. Supreme Court. A writ of error, a proceeding in the nature of an appeal, lay from Common Pleas to King's Bench, and from King's Bench, in turn, to the Court of Exchequer Chamber or to the House of Lords.[34] But as a practical matter, judgments of the common-law courts were almost always final, and the two "higher" courts were extraordinary bodies, rarely invoked and of shifting membership. When reviewing judgments of King's Bench, the Court of Exchequer Chamber consisted of the four judges of Common Pleas and the four barons of the Exchequer.[35] The House of Lords, composed of hereditary peers, when acting as a judicial body was usually guided by the "law lords," a varying number of peers with judicial experience.[36] It was not until the Judicature Acts of 1873–1875 that English appellate

32. 3 WILLIAM BLACKSTONE, COMMENTARIES ON THE LAWS OF ENG-LAND 40–41 (1768). The judges of the Court of Exchequer were called barons, out of a presumed necessity from a provision in Magna Carta. *Id.* at 44.

33. Francis Bacon, *On Judicature, reprinted in* FRANCIS BACON, ESSAYS (1884). *See* 1 Kings 10:20 (KJV).

34. BLACKSTONE, *supra* note 32, at 43.

35. *Id.* at 56.

36. ROBERT STEVENS, LAW AND POLITICS: THE HOUSE OF LORDS AS A JUDICIAL BODY, 1800–1976, at 10–13 (1978).

courts were regularly composed of an odd number of judges: the English Court of Appeal today sits in several divisions of three judges each.[37]

The point here is not that the founders of the common law thought an even number of judges better, but only that they apparently did not think an odd number necessary. In fact, the history of the common law is littered with legal bodies with an even-numbered membership, from the summary courts composed of two justices of the peace,[38] to the solemn circuit courts of two justices of assize, not to mention the venerable jury of twelve "good and lawful men."[39] This fact should give us pause. Perhaps we need to examine exactly why odd numbers leap to our minds today when we are asked how many judges it takes to make a supreme court. Could it be that we have come to expect (and accept) disagreement on legal issues? Could it be that the common law was not always seen as a subject that necessarily lent itself to differences of opinion? Could it be that the drafters of the 1789 Judiciary

37. WALKER, *supra* note 24, at 1199–1200. Of course, an appeal may still be taken from the Court of Appeal to the House of Lords. *Id.* at 585.

38. For examples of summary courts composed of two justices of the peace, see JOHN V. ORTH, COMBINATION AND CONSPIRACY: A LEGAL HISTORY OF TRADE UNIONISM 1721–1906, at 7, 12, 17, 18 (1991). When an early example of labor legislation, the Combination Act of 1799, provided for summary proceedings before one justice of the peace, a storm of protest led to a speedy repeal and reenactment with changes, including a requirement that two justices of the peace hear the case. *Id.* at 52.

39. The time-hallowed phrase appeared in North Carolina's 1776 and 1868 constitutions but was deleted by amendment in 1946 in order to open jury service to women. *See* ORTH, *supra* note 1, at 19, 66.

Act copied the English example of an even number of judges in part because it was not so obvious to them as it is to us that split decisions were to be expected?

Why have multimember courts at all? Why not adopt the model used for chief executives in which final authority is vested in one officer, be it constitutional monarch, president, or governor? The constitution of ancient Sparta with two simultaneous kings remains a lonely monstrosity in world history.[40] And Pennsylvania's early experiment in its 1776 constitution with an executive council of twelve was quickly aborted.[41] The Constitutional Convention in 1787 that produced the "miracle at Philadelphia" was apparently persuaded by James Wilson's argument in favor of a single executive: "A plurality in the Executive of Government would probably produce a tyranny as bad as the thirty Tyrants of Athens, or as the Decemvirs of Rome."[42] Presumably we think executive action may on occasion need to be quick and decisive, the product of one mind.

Shifting the focus of comparison, why not have single-member appellate courts as we now have single-member

40. *See* PLUTARCH, THE LIVES OF THE NOBLE GRECIANS AND ROMANS 53 (Modern Library ed. John Dryden, trans.) (life of Lycurgus).

41. Pa. Const. of 1776, ch. II, § 19, *superseded by* Pa. Const. of 1790. *See* J. PAUL SELSAM, THE PENNSYLVANIA CONSTITUTION OF 1776: A STUDY IN REVOLUTIONARY DEMOCRACY (1971).

42. 1 RECORDS OF THE FEDERAL CONVENTION OF 1787, at 74 (Max Farrand ed. 1911).

trial courts?[43] The English Court of Chancery functioned for most of its history with a single chancellor, as did the Chancery Court of Delaware, the forum in which so many important issues of corporate law were decided.[44] Presumably the answer is because we think a single presiding judge, like a single executive, is better able to make the quick decisions sometimes necessary in the rapid give-and-take of a trial. Indeed, when quick and decisive action is required of an appellate court, a single judge is authorized to act, as with applications for stays.[45] Judging appeals, on the other hand, is viewed as a deliberative process, benefiting from the contributions of many minds. One of Francis Bacon's legal maxims was "Let not these courts be entrusted to the charge of one man, but let them consist of many."[46] "In the multitude of counsellors, there is safety" has been proverbial wisdom since the days of King Solomon.[47]

Many counsellors, of course, do not necessarily mean unanimous counsel; indeed, it is in the very variety of counsel that safety often lies. What must be explained about our

43. It is true that federal circuit courts, which performed both trial and appellate work, were from 1793 to 1869 regularly composed of two judges: a Supreme Court justice and the resident district court judge.

44. The post of vice-chancellor was created in England in 1813, 53 Geo. III, c. 24 (1813), and in Delaware in 1939, 42 Del. Laws c. 148 (1939).

45. *See, e.g.*, U.S. Supreme Court Rule 22.

46. FRANCIS BACON, EXAMPLES OF A TREATISE ON UNIVERSAL JUSTICE (aphorism 38).

47. Proverbs 11:14 (KJV).

view of appellate judging, in other words, is not only the idea that many judges are better than one, but also that an odd number of judges is more eligible than an even one. At the root of the historic shift from an even-numbered to an odd-numbered court seems to lie a changing assumption about whether deliberation on legal subjects by trained judges is likely to result in disagreement. It is the unexamined assumption that often tells us more about what we really believe, and it is the change of assumptions, out of sight and without conscious reflection, that registers the progressions of which we are unaware. In the history of science it is called a "paradigm shift."[48]

A suggestive episode from English legal history casts a chilling light on our contemporary assumption about the value of an odd number of judges. It was King James I in the early seventeenth century who, according to Blackstone, first saw the need for a "casting voice in case of a difference of opinion" and "appointed five judges in every court."[49] The first Stuart monarch is an uncongenial model for American lawyers. A believer in the divine right of kings, James was frequently at odds with his judges and was associated with the dangerous notions that "the Judges are but the delegates of the King" and that "the King may take what causes he

---

48. See THOMAS S. KUHN, THE STRUCTURE OF SCIENTIFIC REVOLUTIONS 175 (2d ed. 1970).

49. BLACKSTONE, supra note 32, at 40 note n.

shall please to determine, from the determination of the Judges and may determine them himself."[50]

On a memorable occasion Sir Edward Coke, chief justice of the Court of Common Pleas, accused the king to his face of proposing to substitute "natural reason" for the "artificial reason and judgment of law," and thereby violate the nascent concept of separation of powers. Coke emphasized that "long study and experience" of the law were required "before that a man can attain to the cognizance of it," suggesting a process of socialization that would minimize differences of opinion.[51] Could it be that the king already perceived law as a matter for individual interpretation and therefore likely to result in divided counsels? James's idea of providing the courts with a "casting voice"—the word *vote* was not yet in vogue where judicial action was involved[52]—was quickly abandoned by his successors, and the stigma of Stuart absolutism that attached to the innovation of a court with an odd number of judges only reinforced English attachment to the traditional four-member courts.

50. 12 Co. Rep. 63, 77 Eng. Rep. 1342 (1608). *See also* CATHERINE DRINKER BOWEN, THE LION AND THE THRONE: THE LIFE AND TIMES OF SIR EDWARD COKE 303 (1957).

51. 12 Co. Rep. 65, 77 Eng. Rep. 1343. *See also* John V. Orth, *Did Sir Edward Coke Mean What He Said?* 16 CONST. COMM. 33, 36–37 (1999).

52. The word *voice* was particularly appropriate in the days when the judges delivered their opinions orally one after the other in a series (seriatim).

Judging between individual litigants on the basis of long-established common-law rules was not particularly likely to lead to disagreements in England in the age of Blackstone, a relatively small and homogeneous society. But in America it was a different matter. Already in 1735 a colonial lawyer had argued that common-law rules on the periphery of the British Empire might not be identical with those at home in England: "What is good law at one time and in one place is not so at another time and in another place."[53] A century later the U.S. Supreme Court itself declared: "The common law of England is not to be taken in all respects to be that of America."[54] Deciding what was and was not appropriate to the changed circumstances of the New World was a question of a different order than deciding what the common law was, and increased the risk of disagreement.

Not only did American courts have to rediscover (if not reinvent) the common law, they also had to construe the requirements of the new written constitutions. "It is emphatically the province and duty of the judicial department to say what the law is," Chief Justice John Marshall intoned in *Marbury v. Madison* with specific reference to constitutional law.[55] This, of course, was to raise the stakes immensely, since custodianship of the constitution would eventually bring the

53. *See* ALEXANDER, *supra* note 26, at 67–68 (argument of Hamilton for defendant).

54. *Van Ness v. Packard,* 27 U.S. (2 Pet.) 137, 144 (1829) (Story, J.).

55. 5 U.S. (1 Cranch) 137 (1803).

judiciary into every part of American life and impinge on the cherished prerogatives of the politicians. So exercised was Thomas Jefferson by the possibility of a decision "perhaps by a majority of one" being presented as the opinion of the court that he thought there ought to be a law requiring the judges publicly to announce their individual opinions seriatim, one after the other, so they would, in effect, have to stand up and be counted.[56]

Akin to the question of how many judges it takes to make a supreme court is the question of the role of the advocates in the decision of an appellate case. Are opposing counsel, as we seem to think today, like gladiators in the ring, contending for a thumbs-up or thumbs-down from the imperial judges? When the common law was assumed to be common knowledge (at least among lawyers), could the advocates once have been seen as collaborators with the judges in the discovery of the law, "officers of the court" in more than name only? Recall that in many early volumes of the U.S. Reports the often lengthy arguments of opposing counsel are set out in full with no obvious break marking the transition to the opinion of the court. In the exchanges between the judges and counsel in the old English Reports it is sometimes even difficult

56. *See* JEAN EDWARD SMITH, JOHN MARSHALL: DEFINER OF A NA-
TION 456 (1996) (quoting letter dated December 25, 1820, from Jefferson
to Thomas Ritchie); *id.* at 662 n. 72 (citing other letters); CHARLES EVANS
HUGHES, THE SUPREME COURT OF THE UNITED STATES 65 (1928) (citing
letter dated March 4, 1823, from Jefferson to William Johnson).

to tell exactly which is which. Could both be "sources of the law"?

As confidence in the obviousness of the rules declined, the importance of the reports as a source of law increased, and the reporters accordingly paid less attention to the arguments of counsel. Does the shift to an exclusive, not to say obsessive, emphasis on the words of the judges reflect our conversion to a highly positivistic view of law? The law is what the judges, and no one else, say it is. Could it be that an earlier generation, not anticipating frequent and endemic disagreements among those "learned in the law," did not understand the law to be solely the will of the judges—or, to be more precise, the will of a majority thereof?

We have, seemingly, moved far beyond the simple question we began with. But the number of judges on our ideal court serves as an index of a much larger issue, our conception of the nature of law itself. To the extent that law is the application of known rules to resolve individual disputes, disagreements among the judges should be relatively rare, and benign—something like medical experts occasionally disagreeing about the proper course of treatment, disagreements that we do not, by the way, necessarily resolve by counting noses. When appellate judging becomes the elaboration of policy as well as, if not more than, the resolution of individual disputes, it inevitably begins to mimic political decision making. Law, in such cases, is the continuation of politics by other means. As the political element comes to predominate, a method is required for the orderly resolution of disagreements, which in our democratic system is ordinarily done by majority vote: each to count for one and only one, although the tradition of judicial opinion writing, explaining the deliberative process, continues to set off judicial decision making from purely majoritarian head counting.[57] Without consciously confronting the question of the nature of law, we nonetheless indicate our likely answer when we supply an answer to the practical question of how many judges it takes to make a supreme court.

57. For a knowledgeable discussion by a former vice-chairman of the Board of Governors of the Federal Reserve system concerning the distinction between politics and technocracy in the practice of American government today, see Alan S. Blinder, *Is Government Too Political?* 76 (no. 6) FOREIGN AFFAIRS 115 (1997).

2

The Secret Sources of Judicial Power

A t least two objections can be made to the topic "The Secret Sources of Judicial Power." The first is that the source of judicial power is not a secret. Judicial power, like all lawful power, comes from the sovereign; in the United States, the sovereign people, who in their several constitutions have vested it in state and federal courts. The U.S. Constitution, Article III, section 1, memorably provides: "The judicial Power of the United States, shall be vested in one supreme Court, and in such inferior Courts as the Congress may from time to time ordain and establish."[1] The language of state constitutions is similar. The Louisiana Constitution, for example, provides: "The judicial power is vested in a supreme court, courts of appeal, district courts, and other courts authorized by this Article."[2] It is noteworthy that the phrase

1. U.S. CONST. art. III, § 1.
2. LA. CONST. art. V, § 1.

"judicial power" is nowhere defined in any of these documents.[3]

The second objection to the topic is that the source of judicial power is, as indicated, single, not multiple. All power is from the people.[4] A particularly clear expression of popular sovereignty is found in the North Carolina Constitution, carried forward verbatim from the state's 1776 Declaration of Rights: "All political power is vested in and derived from the people...."[5] The Louisiana Constitution is to the same effect: "All government, of right, originates with the people [and] is founded on their will alone...."[6] To talk about the sources of judicial power in the plural is to talk about things that do not exist. Both objections may be conceded—up to a point.

Perhaps the emphasis is not really on sources but on power—not the metaphysical power vested in courts by constitutions but the real-world power of enforcing judicial decisions, once made. This would certainly provide an ample subject. Aside from the modest force of United States marshals and state court bailiffs, the judicial power of enforcement lies above all in the voluntary acquiescence of the pub-

---

3. For a study of judicial construction of the words, see William N. Eskridge Jr., *All About Words: Early Understandings of the "Judicial Power" in Statutory Interpretation, 1776–1806*, 101 COLUM. L. REV. 990 (2001).

4. U.S. CONST. preamble.

5. N.C. CONST. art. I, § 2 (repeating N.C. CONST. OF 1776, Declaration of Rights § 1). *See* JOHN V. ORTH, THE NORTH CAROLINA STATE CONSTITUTION: A REFERENCE GUIDE 39–40 (1993).

6. LA. CONST. art. I, § 1.

lic—the sense that even in cases in which we disagree with a decision, we ought to obey it "because it's the law."

Should these sources of power fail, of course, the final resort is to the executive, duty-bound under the various constitutions to "take Care that the Laws be faithfully executed."[7] This is the power that sent federal troops to Little Rock, Arkansas, in 1957 to enforce the U.S. Supreme Court's mandate in *Brown v. Board of Education*.[8] Bluntly stated, it is the power that "grows out of the barrel of a gun."[9] However fascinating that power is, it is not the topic here. I really do want to explore the secret sources of judicial power: power that is peculiarly judicial and sources other than the bare constitutional grants of power, awesome and indispensable as they are.

Judicial power may be defined as the authority to resolve disputes in cases properly before the courts, coupled with the authority to invoke force if necessary to back up those decisions. A final decision in an individual case ends the dispute insofar as the law is concerned. This may be called the *res judicata* effect of the exercise of judicial power. No further legal

7. *See, e.g.,* U.S. CONST. art. II, § 3; N.C. CONST. art. III, § 5, cl. 4. *See also* LA. CONST. art. IV, § 5, cl. A.

8. 347 U.S. 483 (1954). *See* RICHARD KLUGER, SIMPLE JUSTICE: THE HISTORY OF BROWN V. BOARD OF EDUCATION AND BLACK AMERICA'S STRUGGLE FOR EQUALITY 753–754 (1976).

9. QUOTATIONS FROM CHAIRMAN MAO TSE-TUNG 33 (1967) ("the little red book"). Actually, the people of the United States generally respond to displays of federal force not only because of the firepower but also because of the perceived legitimacy of the armed services.

action between the same parties concerning the same dispute is permitted: it has become "a thing adjudged."

Notice that nothing more than an enforceable decision between two disputants is involved in the bare exercise of judicial power. A judgment must be rendered that is intelligible to those involved, and a sufficient record must be made to ensure enforcement if necessary and to prevent relitigation if attempted.[10] This record need not be kept by the court itself, although it usually is. It could be kept by the parties: the winner, for enforcement actions; the loser, to prevent further suit. The records routinely kept by courts are not so much for the convenience of the parties as for the convenience of the judicial system; they provide institutional memory for the deciding court and material for review by higher courts or other branches of government. The practical problem of authenticating records held by private parties, although not insurmountable, is another reason for maintaining public records.

Since the first principle of justice is that "like cases should be decided alike,"[11] the decision in an individual case is of interest to more than the parties involved. In a later case, if the facts are sufficiently similar (and if the judges do not decide

10. *Court of record* is a technical term in the history of English law, signifying courts that kept records on parchment in Latin and that alone had power to fine and imprison. *See* 5 WILLIAM HOLDSWORTH, HISTORY OF ENGLISH LAW 157–161 (3d ed. 1945); S. E. Thorne, *Courts of Record and Sir Edward Coke*, 11 U. TORONTO L.J. 24 (1937). In this essay court records are used in the ordinary, nontechnical sense.

11. *See* 2 EDWARD COKE, COMMENTARY UPON LITTLETON § 301, at 191a (1628) ("wheresoever there is the like reason, there is the like law").

to reconsider their original resolution), the result should be the same. This is the common-law doctrine of precedent and may be labeled the *stare decisis* effect of the exercise of judicial power; the judges' collective resolve "to stand by [their] decisions," in the sense of standing by the general propositions of law that have been established.[12] To operate effectively, stare decisis requires some kind of record; again, not necessarily a public record but one that subsequent courts will accept as evidence of prior judicial action. In addition, such a record promotes judicial efficiency by saving the judges from having to think through every issue anew and minimizes the potential institutional embarrassment of giving the same question different answers.

In the common-law world, the most familiar records of judicial action are the "reports." Reporting of a sort began very early with the Year Books—so early, in fact, that they were written in French, the language of English courts for centuries after the Norman Conquest in 1066. More recognizable law reports began to appear in the sixteenth century, particularly the immensely influential reports prepared by Sir

12. Because of its civil law background, Louisiana applies the concept expressed by the French phrase *jurisprudence constante* rather than *stare decisis*. Louisiana courts need not recognize a rule established by a single judicial decision; only when courts have consistently applied it does a rule become binding. See A. N. YIANNOPOULOS, LOUISIANA CIVIL LAW SYSTEM § 35, at 53–56 (1977); James L. Dennis, *Interpretation and Application of the Civil Code and the Evolution of Judicial Precedent*, 54 LA. L. REV. I, 15 (1993). Like *stare decisis, jurisprudence constante* requires accessible records for its effectiveness.

Edward Coke, long called simply "the Reports."[13] For hundreds of years, law reports accumulated, most of them available today in the monumental series of English Reports—Full Reprint. Prepared by individual lawyers or judges, they were essentially private-enterprise undertakings, not official reports in the modern sense. At first, they were published only if and when the author, or the representative of a deceased author, saw an opportunity for fame or profit.[14]

Different reporters covered the same courts and periods, resulting in multiple reports of the same cases, not all of them alike. Dyer's reports of decisions in the Court of King's Bench from 1537 to 1582[15] may be usefully compared with the reports of Plowden, who covered the same court for the years 1550 to 1580.[16] When the common law was assumed to be common knowledge, there was no particular reason to look to the law reports for the rules, except for the complex rules governing real property, which is why the early reporters focused on procedural niceties—and such exotica as the Rule in Shelley's Case[17] and the Rule in Wild's Case.[18]

13. 1–13 Co. Rep., 76–77 Eng. Rep. *See* DAVID M. WALKER, THE OXFORD COMPANION TO LAW 1059 (1980).

14. *See* WILLIAM GELDART, INTRODUCTION OF ENGLISH LAW 5 (D. C. M. Yardley ed., 9th ed. 1984).

15. 1–3 Dy., 73 Eng. Rep.

16. 1–2 Pl. Com., 75 Eng. Rep.

17. 1 Co. Rep. 93b, 76 Eng. Rep. 206 (C.P. 1581). *See also* John V. Orth, *The Mystery of the Rule in Shelley's Case*, 7 GREEN BAG 2D 45 (2003).

18. 6 Co. Rep. 16b, 77 Eng. Rep. 277 (K.B. 1599). *See also* Ronald Link, *The Rule in Wild's Case in North Carolina*, 55 N.C. L. REV. 751 (1977).

Reports varied considerably in quality with the skill, understanding, and attentiveness of the respective reporters. In a 1704 case, Lord Holt, chief justice of the Court of King's Bench, described the so-called Modern Reports, covering decisions of his own court, as "scambling reports" that "will make us appear to posterity for a parcel of blockheads,"[19] and Dr. Johnson rated the English Reports in general "very poor: only half of what has been said is taken down; and of that half, much is mistaken."[20] In the nineteenth century, Lord Lyndhurst, the lord chancellor, recalled that "in my younger days, it was said of [Thomas] Barnardiston [who published reports of Chancery decisions in 1740 and 1741], that he was accustomed to slumber over his note-book, and the wags in the rear took the opportunity of scribbling nonsense in it."[21] The picture, of course, is comical, but the cost in terms of the reliability of the reports and the consequent effectiveness of precedent is serious. As confidence in the obviousness of the rules declined, the importance of the reports as a source of law increased, and the reporters accordingly paid more attention to the rules laid down in the cases. The reports became, in effect, a source of positive law—a very special form of legislation.

19. *Slater v. May*, 2 Ld. Raym. 1071, 92 Eng. Rep. 210, 210 (K.B. 1704) (referring to 4 Mod., 87 Eng. Rep. (K.B.)).

20. 1 JAMES BOSWELL, LIFE OF SAMUEL JONSON (Rodney Shewan ed. 1968) (first published 1791).

21. *Quoted in* JOHN WILLIAM WALLACE, THE REPORTERS: ARRANGED AND CHARACTERIZED WITH INCIDENTAL REMARKS 424 (4th ed. 1882).

Lord Mansfield, the great chief justice of King's Bench from 1756 to 1788, used the freedom to doubt the old reports as a source of power as he reshaped English law, particularly in the commercial field. "Their [*sic*] being no solemn well-considered decision," as he put it in one case, "we must resort to principles,"[22] that is, despite the five-hundred-year-long history of his court, he could treat the matter as one of first instance. But while the absence of reliable reports gave Mansfield power in his own day, their continued absence risked diminishing his power in the future, if his successors were as free to doubt the reports of his court as he had been to doubt those of his predecessors.

The solution was the development of reliable reports published contemporaneously with the decisions, and Mansfield found the reporter he needed in James Burrow, who set a new professional standard by keeping meticulous records.[23] A connoisseur of reports described them as "works of art."[24] Having increased his judicial power by doubting prior reports, Mansfield increased it yet again by creating reports that could not be doubted. Like all historical transitions, particularly in so traditional a culture as English law, the victory of professional reporting was not immediate. John Campbell, later Lord Campbell, who, as a young lawyer, compiled

---

22. *Eaton v. Jaques,* 2 Dougl. 455, 460, 99 Eng. Rep. 290, 292 (K.B. 1780).

23. *See* HOLDSWORTH, *supra* note 10, at 110–112.

24. *See* WALLACE, *supra* note 21.

reports of *nisi prius* decisions from 1808 to 1816, was less than completely honest: we are told that "he kept a drawer marked 'Bad Law' into which he threw all the cases which seemed to him 'improperly ruled.'"[25] But the move to professional reporting was unstoppable. The establishment in 1865 of the Incorporated Council on Law Reporting made the following of precedents appreciably more systematic.[26]

In America, the first court reporters, like their English counterparts, were volunteers, preparing reports for sale. François-Xavier Martin, for instance, reported decisions of the superior courts of North Carolina from 1778 to 1797,[27] as did other aspiring lawyers. When the current volume 1 of the North Carolina Reports was prepared in modern times, duplication was avoided by omitting reports prepared by John Haywood, Archibald Murphey, and other distinguished lawyers.[28] Not only did Martin, like his English counterpart, have competitors, but like them, he also saw no reason to refrain from editorial comments. Reporting an episode in one of North Carolina's most important early cases, *Bayard*

---

25. Gareth Jones, *Three Very Remarkable Nineteenth-Century Lawyers: Lyndhurst, Denman, and Campbell, in* HUMAN RIGHTS AND LEGAL HISTORY: ESSAYS IN HONOUR OF BRIAN SIMPSON 172, 177 (Katherine O'Donovan & Gerry R. Rubins eds. 2000).

26. BRIAN ABEL-SMITH & ROBERT STEVENS, LAWYERS AND THE COURTS: A SOCIOLOGICAL STUDY OF THE ENGLISH LEGAL SYSTEM 46–47 (1967).

27. 1 N.C. (1–2 Mart.) (1778–1797).

28. *See* 1 N.C. preface.

v. Singleton,[29] which established judicial review under the state constitution fifteen years before *Marbury v. Madison,*[30] Martin testily concluded: "This [Judge Samuel Ashe] said without disclosing a single sentiment upon the cause of the proceeding, or the law introduced in support of it."[31] Martin later migrated to the Territory of Orleans, becoming Louisiana's first attorney general and later judge and chief justice of the Louisiana Supreme Court, as well as reporting the decisions of the Louisiana courts from 1809 to 1830.[32]

The U.S. Supreme Court appointed its first official reporter in 1816,[33] but he too relied largely on private sales for his compensation, one reason the early U.S. Reports, like the English Reports, are known to law librarians as "nominative," that is, cited by the reporters' last names: Dallas, Cranch, Wheaton, and so on. Chief Justice John Marshall took great care with his opinions, explaining the decisions at length and aiming to persuade and educate the public as well as the parties; in a celebrated instance, he even published an anonymous defense of one of his own decisions in a news-

29. 1 N.C. (1 Mart.) 5, 5 (1787).

30. 5 U.S. (1 Cranch) 137 (1803).

31. 1 N.C. (1 Mart.) 5, 5 (1787). *See also* John V. Orth, *"Fundamental Principles" in North Carolina Constitutional History,* 69 N.C. L. Rev. 1357, 1357–1358 (1991).

32. 1–3 La. (1–12 Mart. (o.s.)) (1818–1823); 4-5 La. (1–8 Mart. (n.s.)) (1823–1830).

33. 1 Charles Warren, The Supreme Court in United States History 455 (1922). An annual salary of $1,000 was authorized by the Act of March 3, 1817, ch. 63, 3 Stat. 376.

paper.[34] But it was Justice Joseph Story, Marshall's learned
protégé, who took a particular interest in the accuracy of the
reports.[35] In this regard, perhaps, it should come as no surprise that Story, despite his esteem for Chief Justice Marshall, took Lord Mansfield as his judicial hero.[36]

That accurate and available reports are a source of judicial
power is demonstrated by the career of James Kent, chancellor of New York from 1814 to 1823, and subsequently author
of the classic *Commentaries on American Law*. Kent, whose
decisions were well reported by William Johnson, laid the
foundations of American equity jurisprudence during his
tenure as chancellor but later recalled that "for the nine years
I was in that office there was not a single decision, opinion,
or dictum of either of my two predecessors..., from 1777 to
1814, cited to me or even suggested."[37] The judicial power of
New York had undoubtedly been fully vested in the state's
first chancellors and was assuredly exercised by them, but to
no discernible effect beyond the individual litigants.

34. *See* JOHN MARSHALL'S DEFENSE of McCULLOCH v. MARYLAND 78
(Gerald Gunther ed. 1969).

35. Craig Joyce, *The Rise of the Supreme Court Reporter: An Institutional
Perspective on Marshall Court Ascendancy,* 83 MICH. L. REV. 1291, 1320–1321
(1985).

36. R. KENT NEWMYER, SUPREME COURT JUSTICE JOSEPH STORY:
STATESMAN OF THE OLD REPUBLIC 246 (1985).

37. MEMOIRS AND LETTERS OF JAMES KENT 157–158 (William Kent ed.
1898). Kent claimed that earlier he had been the first to introduce written
opinions in the New York Supreme Court. *Id.* 117.

The common law, of course, was made by judges who did more than simply resolve disputes; they customarily explained their decisions in some kind of opinion as well.[38] How they expressed themselves is worth noting. Since the inception of the common law, English judges delivered their opinions in each case speaking one after another in series, seriatim. They still do, as do all common-law judges around the world, except in America. But for a brief period of time shortly before American independence Lord Mansfield persuaded his colleagues (properly known as *puisne* judges) to permit the court to speak with one voice.[39] Like the newly reliable reports published by Burrow, the unitary opinion of the court was a potential source of judicial power. The court's holding was less equivocal; indeed, it was quite literally univocal. No longer did one have to grapple with multiple rationales delivered by several judges in the same case. Even the great Mansfield, however, was unable to hold his colleagues in line; seriatim opinions soon reappeared. Perhaps the puisnes felt that their judicial individuality was being lost. More likely, the force of tradition was just too strong; it is, after all, easier in a traditional society to improve on tradition, as with better-quality reports, than to dispense with tradition altogether.

The "opinion of the court" was to become the standard form of American judicial expression. While not quite the

38. *Cf. Goldberg v. Kelly*, 397 U.S. 254, 255 (1970) (requiring as an element of due process a statement of the reasons for a decision).

39. *See* Lawrence Friedman, A History of American Law 117 (1973).

invention of John Marshall, it owes its present canonical status to him. From the first organization of the U.S. Supreme Court in 1790 until Marshall's appointment as its head in 1801, the justices conformed to English practice and delivered their opinions one after the other.[40] For example, in *Chisholm v. Georgia*,[41] the 1793 case asserting federal jurisdiction over suits by private individuals against states, the justices delivered their opinions in reverse order of seniority, with Justice James Iredell of North Carolina, the sole dissenter, speaking first—to the consternation of modern-day law students![42]

Under Marshall's leadership, the Court literally found a new voice, usually his own, and typically issued only one opinion. Thomas Jefferson, an astute lawyer and politician in his own right, recognized the profound significance of the change and thought there ought to be a law requiring the judges to announce their separate opinions in the English fashion—a rare instance of Jefferson preferring English tradition to American innovation.[43] The Louisiana legislature

40. The increasing appearance of per curiam opinions during this period pointed the way ahead. *See* GEORGE L. HASKINS & HERBERT A. JOHNSON, FOUNDATIONS OF POWER: JOHN MARSHALL, 1801–15, at 382–389 (1981), vol. 2 of OLIVER WENDELL HOLMES DEVISE HISTORY OF THE SUPREME COURT OF THE UNITED STATES.

41. 2 U.S. (2 Dall.) 419 (1793). *See* JOHN V. ORTH, THE JUDICIAL POWER OF THE UNITED STATES: THE ELEVENTH AMENDMENT IN AMERICAN HISTORY 12–29 (1987).

42. For an analysis of Iredell's dissent, see John V. Orth, *The Truth about Justice Iredell's Dissent in Chisholm v. Georgia*, 73 N.C. L. REV. 255 (1994).

43. JEAN EDWARD SMITH, JOHN MARSHALL: DEFINER OF A NATION 456 (1996) (quoting letter dated December 25, 1820, from Jefferson to

had the same idea at about the same time, passing a statute that required the judges of the state supreme court to deliver *seriatim* opinions,[44] but the requirement was mocked by the judges, who serially concurred in the principal opinion "for the reasons adduced." The legislature repealed the statute the following year.[45]

So thoroughly did Jefferson lose this particular battle and so fully were the judges aware of the extent to which judicial power was enhanced by presenting a united front that a norm of unanimity developed. Justice William Johnson, who sought to express his own views in dissent, plaintively wrote to Jefferson: "During the rest of the Session I heard nothing but Lectures on the Indecency of Judges cutting at each other, and the Loss of Reputation which the Virginia appellate Court had sustained by pursuing such a Course."[46] Years later, Oliver Wendell Holmes remarked that dissenting was considered rude, as if the dissenter were telling the

---

Thomas Ritchie); *id.* at 662 n. 72 (citing other letters); CHARLES EVANS HUGHES, THE SUPREME COURT OF THE UNITED STATES 65 (1928) (citing letter dated March 4, 1823, from Jefferson to William Johnson). *See also* Julian S. Waterman, *Thomas Jefferson and Blackstone's Commentaries,* 27 ILL. L. REV. 629 (1933).

44. Act of Feb. 17, 1821, § 2, 1821 La. Acts, at 98 (repealed 1822).

45. Act of Feb. 27, 1822, § 3, 1822 La. Acts, at 24. *See* Henry Plauche Dart, *The History of the Louisiana Supreme Court, in* 133 La. xxx, at xxxviii (1913).

46. Letter dated Dec. 10, 1822, from Johnson to Jefferson, *quoted in* Donald G. Morgan, *Mr. Justice William Johnson and the Constitution,* 57 HARV. L. REV. 328, 333 (1944).

majority they had not done their sums right.[47] But more was at stake than judicial propriety; judicial power was also implicated. "It is of high importance," the American Bar Association (ABA) formally announced in 1924, "that judges constituting a court of last resort should use effort and self restraint to promote solidarity of conclusion."[48] Canon 19 of the ABA's code of judicial conduct, unaltered until 1972, cautioned judges not to yield to "pride of opinion" and enjoined that, "[e]xcept in cases of conscientious difference of opinion on fundamental principle, dissenting opinions should be discouraged."[49] The Louisiana Constitutions of 1898 and 1913 actually prohibited the publication of dissenting or concurring opinions;[50] but the reports amply show that the prohibition was disregarded by the judges, and the 1921 Constitution did not repeat the provision.[51]

47. O. W. Holmes, *The Path of the Law,* 10 HARV. L. REV. 457, 465 (1897).

48. ABA CANONS OF JUDICIAL ETHICS CANON 19 (1924), *reprinted in* LISA L. MILORD, THE DEVELOPMENT OF THE ABA JUDICIAL CODE 137 (1992).

49. *Id. See generally* Robert Post, *The Supreme Court Opinion as Institutional Practice: Dissent, Legal Scholarship, and Decisionmaking in the Taft Court,* 85 MINN. L. REV. 1267 (2001).

50. LA. CONST. of 1898, art. 92; LA. CONST. of 1913, art. 92; LA. CONST. of 1921, art. 92.

51. *See* Symeon C. Symeonides, *The Louisiana Judge: Judge, Statesman, Politician, in* LOUISIANA: MICROCOSM OF A MIXED JURISDICTION 89, 95 (Vernon Valentine Palmer ed. 1999) (citing cases disregarding the prohibition).

Judicial power is the power to resolve disputes. It is fully exercised even by courts deciding without opinion, as in summary affirmances per curiam, or without published opinion.[52] But for the judges to exert power beyond the individual dispute, they must explain themselves and make their explanations available to a wide audience. Hence the development of reliable law reports and the emergence, at least in America, of the solitary opinion of the court. Note, by the way, how this characteristic of judicial power contrasts with legislative and executive power: the political branches do much of their work—and some of what they regard as their best work—in obscurity. The judicial power, by contrast, grows greater as it becomes more widely known.[53] This is one of the most appealing aspects of judicial power and a chief reason why the judicial branch is the least dangerous.[54]

In interaction with civil law systems, the power of common-law precedent can work wonders. Lord Mansfield, a na-

---

52. See *Anastasoff v. United States*, 223 F.3d 898 (8th Cir. 2000) (holding unconstitutional the judicial practice of denying precedential effect to unpublished opinions). *See also* Polly J. Price, *Precedent and Judicial Power after the Founding*, 42 B.C. L. REV. 81 (2000); Carl Tobias, *Anastasoff, Unpublished Opinions, and Federal Appellate Justice*, 25 HARV. L. & PUB. POL'Y 1171 (2002).

53. Francis Bacon believed that requiring the judges to make a public statement of the reasons for their decisions helped to maintain judicial standards: "[W]hat is free in point of power may yet be restrained by regard to character and reputation." EXAMPLES OF A TREATISE ON UNIVERSAL JUSTICE (aphorism 38).

54. See Alexander Hamilton, THE FEDERALIST No. 78. *But see* ALEXANDER BICKEL, THE LEAST DANGEROUS BRANCH 1 (1962).

tive of Scotland, a mixed common-law–civil-law jurisdiction
like Louisiana, drew on his extensive knowledge of foreign
law as he brought the common law into the modern world
of commerce.[55] Critics, including Thomas Jefferson, charged
Mansfield with judicial activism.[56] More recently in America, Judge J. Skelly Wright, educated in Louisiana, rewrote
the common law of landlord and tenant with the recognition
of an implied warranty of habitability in residential leases:
"The civil law has always viewed the lease as a contract," he
observed in a landmark case, citing Louisiana's Civil Code,
"and in our judgment that perspective has proved superior to
that of the common law."[57] What began as a code provision
ended up as a common-law precedent and spread rapidly to
a large majority of American states.[58] In what may become

55. *See* HOLDSWORTH, *supra* note 10, at 555–560.

56. *See* Thomas Jefferson, Letter to Philip Mazzei (Nov. 28, 1785), *re-printed in* 9 THE PAPERS OF THOMAS JEFFERSON 67, 71 (Julian P. Boyd ed. 1954); *see also* Letter XLI (Nov. 14, 1770) by the pseudonymous English critic Junius, *reprinted in* THE LETTERS OF JUNIUS 206, 209–210 (John Cannon ed. 1978).

57. *Javins v. First National Realty Corp.*, 428 F.2d 1071, 1075 n. 13 (D.C. Cir. 1970) (citing La. Civ. Code Ann. art. 2669). Judge Wright also au-thored the equally pathbreaking decisions in *Edwards v. Habib*, 397 F.2d 687 (D.C. Cir. 1968) (concerning retaliatory eviction) and *Robinson v. Dia-mond Housing Corp.*, 463 F.2d 853 (D.C. Cir. 1972) (same).

58. *See* JOHN E. CRIBBET ET AL., CASES AND MATERIALS ON PROPERTY 433 (8th ed. 2002). *See, e.g.*, North Carolina Residential Rental Agreements Act, N.C. Gen. Stat. §§ 42-38 to 42-46. *See also* John V. Orth, *Who Is a Ten-ant? The Correct Definition of the Status in North Carolina*, 21 N.C. CENT. L.J. 79, 79–84 (1995); John V. Orth, *Confusion Worse Confounded: The Resi-dential Rental Agreements Act*, 78 N.C. L. REV. 783, 783–797 (2000).

yet another example, the latest Restatement of the Law of Servitudes has adopted the Louisiana rule concerning the relocation of easements,[59] to the dismay of some property scholars trained in the common law.[60] Should it find general acceptance in the courts, the civil law would again propagate by common-law methods.

Without precedents, the common law is like the civil law without the code. Promoting his first volume of U.S. Supreme Court Reports in 1812, William Cranch explained: "Much of that uncertainty of the law, which is so frequently, and perhaps so justly, the subject of complaint in this country, may be attributed to the want of American reports."[61] Lack of accessible local reports causes judges to rely on published reports from other jurisdictions, with serious consequences. A historian of Australian law asserts that a nascent common law in that country was aborted, at least in part, because of "the poor state of legal reporting." "The colonial judges," he said, "tended to look only to English legal decisions, not to those of their colleagues in other colonies."[62]

---

59. RESTATEMENT (THIRD) OF PROP.: SERVITUDES § 4.8(3) (2000); *id.* cmt. f, at 563; *id.* Reporter's note, at 575 (citing La. Civ. Code Ann. art. 748). *See also* Susan F. French, *Relocating Easements: Restatement (Third), Servitudes § 4.8(3),* 38 REAL PROP. PROB. & TR. J. 1 (2003).

60. *See, e.g.,* John V. Orth, *Relocating Easements: A Response to Professor French,* 38 REAL PROP. PROB. & TR. J. 643 (2004).

61. 5 U.S. (1 Cranch) preface (1812).

62. BRUCE KERCHER, AN UNRULY CHILD 93 (1995). In addition to "the poor state of legal reporting," Kercher attributes the demise of an Australian common law to "[t]he dominant belief by the second half of the nine-

Reliable law reports and unequivocal opinions enhance judicial power. They are secret sources of power in the sense that they are generally unobserved. In fact, they go unnoticed because so obvious, like the incriminating document in Edgar Allan Poe's famous short story "The Purloined Letter," hidden in plain view. The battle for reliable reports today is won; the only remaining problem is that official reporters, dependent on government bureaus for publication, are unable to meet the legal community's demand for instant information. Private-enterprise reporters like the West Publishing Company, energized by the profit motive and using the latest technology, are with us yet.

The victory represented by the unitary opinion of the court, however, is not so certain. Drawn to express their individual opinions on every issue, torn by political differences, reacting to the inherent complexity of the problems posed by modern litigation, today's appellate judges are less willing to unite in a single statement and, therefore, frequently produce opinions that are opinions of the court in name only and in fact represent the views of a plurality or even, in some cases, a minority of the judges. Not only have multiple opinions proliferated, but the standards of judicial propriety have crumbled under the pressure of divisive social issues. In one case concerning affirmative action,[63] the judges of the Sixth Circuit Court of

---

teenth century that there was one, universal, timeless common law, and that colonial conditions would rarely justify its non-acceptance."

63. *Grutter v. Bollinger*, 288 F.3d 732 (6th Cir. 2002).

Appeals hurled accusations of misconduct at one another, while in an advisory opinion concerning same-sex marriage delivered by the justices of the once-staid Massachusetts Supreme Judicial Court, Chief Justice Margaret Marshall wrote that a fellow justice's opinion "so clearly misses the point that further discussion appears to be useless."[64]

In a substantive sense, judicial power can also be greatly enhanced if wielded by an expert. One of the less recognized elements of John Marshall's greatness is that he took an institution seemingly destined for insignificance and made it, to a remarkable degree, a coequal branch of the national government, and he did so using only materials ready to hand. In 1801, President John Adams, searching for an appointee to fill the then-vacant chief justiceship, inquired of John Jay, who had resigned as the nation's first chief justice in 1795, if he would accept reappointment. Would he be the once and future chief justice? Jay refused, probably mindful of *Chisholm* and its ignominious reversal by constitutional amendment. "I left the bench," he gloomily replied to the president, "perfectly convinced that under a system so defective it would not obtain the energy, weight, and dignity which are essential to its affording due support to the national government, nor acquire the public confidence and respect which, as the last resort of the justice of the nation, it should possess."[65] Mar-

---

64. Opinion of the Justices, 802 N.E.2d 565 (Mass. 2004).

65. Letter dated Jan. 2, 1801 from Jay to Adams, *quoted in* 3 ALBERT J. BEVERIDGE, THE LIFE OF JOHN MARSHALL 55 (1919).

shall took the job, his first judicial appointment, and brought to it an apparently instinctive understanding of the nature of judicial power.[66]

In *Marbury v. Madison*[67] in 1803 and *United States v. Burr*[68] in 1807, the new chief justice confronted the daunting prospect of issuing orders to the executive branch of government, potentially the most difficult orders for a court to enforce. In *Marbury*, an original action in the Supreme Court, the plaintiffs petitioned the Court to issue a writ of mandamus to Secretary of State James Madison ordering him to produce their commissions for the office of justice of the peace in the District of Columbia. In *Burr*, the prosecution of former vice president Aaron Burr for the crime of treason against the United States, the defendant moved that a subpoena *duces tecum* be served on President Thomas Jefferson, requiring him to appear and produce documents allegedly necessary to the defense. In both cases, the political context indicated that the executive officers in question would be extremely reluctant to comply with the requested orders. In *Marbury*, the Court declined to issue the mandamus for reasons set forth by Marshall in the opinion of the Court. In *Burr*, by contrast, the chief justice, presiding at the trial in the Circuit Court for the District of Virginia, seemed to relish the prospect of

66. Actually, Marshall had held a minor judicial post in Richmond from 1785 to 1788. SMITH, *supra* note 43, at 105.

67. 5 U.S. (1 Cranch) 137 (1803).

68. 25 F. Cas. 2 (C.C.D. Va. 1807) (No. 14,692a).

subpoenaing the president. In both cases, Marshall showed virtuosic mastery in the exercise of judicial power.

Of course, *Marbury v. Madison* is known today as the case that established judicial review, the doctrine that the U.S. Supreme Court is the final authority on the constitutionality of the acts of the other branches of government.[69] Yet, when first filed, the case seemed more likely to diminish judicial power than enhance it. Had the Court ruled for the plaintiffs and issued the requested order, and had the executive officer then refused to obey it, the Court, already so enfeebled in the estimation of former chief justice John Jay, would have suffered yet another humiliating defeat. On the other hand, for the Court to deny the request on the ground that it lacked the power to force the executive to comply with its order would have been still worse: an executive officer, not answerable to a court, would be above the law.

Instead, led by Marshall, the Court refused to resolve the dispute on the ground that it lacked jurisdiction; in other words, judicial power could not be invoked by the plaintiffs because the case was not properly before the Court.[70] There

69. Although *Marbury* is widely credited as the case that established judicial review, the doctrine was implicit in a number of earlier decisions. *See* David P. Currie, The Constitution in the Supreme Court: The First Hundred Years, 1789–1888, at 6–7, 20, 22–23, 30, 39–42, 51–54 (1985). It is not my purpose here to enter into the debate as to which really the first such case.

70. There presumably was some court in which the suit could be brought, but in fact the plaintiffs commenced no further proceedings. For further discussion of *Marbury*, see Orth, *supra* note 41, at 30–34.

may even be a quibble about whether judicial power was exercised at all, since no dispute was resolved, although that did not stop the chief justice from reading the secretary of state an extensive lecture on the justice of the plaintiffs' claim—all dicta, of course. The remarkable feat performed by Marshall's opinion in *Marbury* was to explain the Court's lack of jurisdiction in terms that actually amounted to a claim to the highest legal power in the nation. Marshall said the Court lacked jurisdiction over the dispute, despite the fact that the Judiciary Act, as he read it, actually purported to give the Court that power.[71]

Comparing the act's supposed grant of jurisdiction with Article III's grant of judicial power, Marshall concluded that the legislation was nothing less than an attempt by Congress to extend the Court's jurisdiction beyond constitutional

71. Marshall read the relevant sentence in the Judiciary Act as an attempt to confer on the Supreme Court the power to issue writs of mandamus in original actions, such as *Marbury*. To reach that result, he elided parts of the sentence, resulting in: "The Supreme Court ... shall have power to issue ... writs of mandamus. ..." Read as a whole, the sentence could just as easily (and perhaps more naturally) have been meant to limit the power to cases in the appellate jurisdiction of the Court: "The Supreme Court shall also have *appellate jurisdiction* from the circuit courts and courts of the several states, in the cases herein after specially provided for; and shall have power to issue writs of prohibition to the district courts, when proceeding as courts of admiralty and maritime jurisdiction, and writs of mandamus, in cases warranted by the principles and usages of law, to any courts appointed, or persons holding office, under the authority of the United States." Judiciary Act of 1789, § 13, 1 Stat. 73, 81 (italics added). *See* John J. Gibbons, *The Interdependence of Legitimacy: An Introduction to the Meaning of Separation of Powers,* 5 SETON HALL L. REV. 435, 437–453 (1974).

limits.[72] In a supreme (and supremely ironic) act of self-denial, the Court piously refused to accept this grant of power. In fact, *Marbury* could be read as a purely defensive use of the power of judicial review, protecting the Court from the constitutional violation supposedly authorized by the Judiciary Act, although in legal tradition it has always been thought to stand for a much greater prerogative.[73] In the specific facts of *Marbury,* the decision was self-enforcing, since no other branch of government could act, or make the Court act, in this case. Implicitly, of course, the chief justice was also announcing that the Court alone among the branches could decide on constitutionality, the *ne plus ultra* of judicial power. As a matter of fact, the Marshall Court never again declared an act of Congress unconstitutional. The next exercise of this awesome power was in the infamous *Dred Scott* case in 1857 when Chief Justice Roger Taney squandered the judicial capital accumulated by Marshall in the defense of slavery.[74]

72. The Constitution limits the Supreme Court's original jurisdiction to a certain number of specific cases, not including cases like *Marbury:* "In all Cases affecting Ambassadors, other public Ministers and Consuls, and those in which a State shall be a Party, the supreme Court shall have original Jurisdiction. In all the other Cases before mentioned, the supreme Court shall have appellate Jurisdiction, both as to Law and Fact, with such Exceptions, and under such Regulations as the Congress shall make." U.S. CONST. art. III, § 2, cl. 2.

73. In this regard, *Marbury* resembles *Bayard,* the North Carolina case establishing judicial review under the state constitution: the judges in *Bayard* refused to abandon traditional judicial procedure, trial by jury, at the command of the legislature.

74. 60 U.S. (19 How.) 393 (1857). *See generally* DON E. FEHRENBACHER,

If the dynamics in *Marbury* were at least in part concerned with the Supreme Court's fear of executive defiance, the trial court in the treason trial of Aaron Burr seemed not to share such fear. When the defendant requested the court to subpoena the president, Marshall showed no undue alarm. President Jefferson had issued a proclamation warning the nation against the treasonous machinations of the former vice president, declaring that Burr's guilt was "placed beyond question."[75] The president had also disclosed parts of certain letters from Burr addressed to General James Wilkinson in New Orleans that seemed to implicate the defendant in plans to separate the Western territories from the United States.[76] Burr requested that Jefferson be compelled to appear at the trial to submit to cross-examination and that he produce the originals of the documents in question.[77] The president was clearly unwilling to comply, yet he was just as clearly unwilling to defy the order and instructed the federal prosecutor to accommodate as many of the court's demands as possible. In the end, the matter was rendered moot as Marshall, distinguishing a decision he himself had only recently authored, so narrowly construed the constitutional definition of treason that the jury acquitted Burr.[78]

THE DRED SCOTT CASE: ITS SIGNIFICANCE IN AMERICAN LAW AND POLITICS (1978).

75. HASKINS & JOHNSON, *supra* note 40, at 254.

76. *United States v. Burr*, 25 F. Cas. 30, 31 (C.C.D. Va. 1807) (No. 14,692d).

77. *Id.* at 30.

78. *Id.* at 55, 59–80 (C.C.D. Va. 1807) (No. 14,693) (distinguishing Ex parte Bollman, 8 U.S. (4 Cranch) 75 (1807)). On Burr's conspiracy and

Why was the Supreme Court under Marshall's leadership in *Marbury* so wary of challenging the secretary of state,
while the circuit court, also under Marshall's headship in
Burr, seemed unafraid of taking on the president himself?
The answer lies in the nature of judicial power, as Marshall
implicitly understood. Comprehensively defined, judicial
power is the legal authority to resolve disputes in appropriate
cases. As such, it encompasses both civil suits like *Marbury*
and criminal prosecutions like *Burr.* In criminal cases, the
government is seeking the authority of a judicial judgment to
apply punishment to the accused. However much Jefferson
wanted to punish Burr—and he instructed the prosecutor
to go to "*any* expense"[79]—he could do so lawfully only with
the court's approval. At an early stage of the trial, Marshall
apparently thought the president needed to be reminded of
that fact, angrily denying that "the hand of malignity [pre-
sumably Jefferson's] may grasp any individual against whom
its hate may be directed, or whom it may capriciously seize,
charge him with some secret crime, and put him on the proof
of his innocence."[80] The executive needed the court in *Burr*

---

the Territory of Orleans, see GEORGE DARGO, JEFFERSON'S LOUISIANA:
POLITICS AND THE CLASH OF LEGAL TRADITIONS 51–73 (1975). For an ac-
count of the entire "Burr conspiracy," see BUCKNER F. MELTON JR., AARON
BURR: CONSPIRACY TO TREASON (2002).

79. Instruction from Thomas Jefferson to George Hay, *quoted in* RICH-
ARD B. MORRIS, FAIR TRIAL: FOURTEEN WHO STOOD ACCUSED, FROM
ANNE HUTCHINSON TO ALGER HISS 129 (1952) (italics in original).

80. *United States v. Burr,* 25 F. Cas. 2, 12 (C.C.D. Va. 1807) (No.
14,692a).

to accomplish its ends, so it had meekly to accept the rebuke and abide by the court's rules. In *Marbury*, on the contrary, the court would have needed executive compliance had it taken the case and found in favor of the plaintiffs. Marshall shrewdly guided the fledgling Supreme Court to avoid the risk of executive defiance, at the same time using the case to make a clear statement of the power of judicial review.

Power is as power does, and resourceful judges have long understood how to maximize judicial power. Courts are essentially reactive bodies, to which disputes are brought for resolution, but this apparent weakness may conceal secret sources of strength. Courts decide whether they have jurisdiction, whether a dispute is justiciable, whether parties have standing, whether an issue is ripe, and whether an appeal is interlocutory. In cases that are taken for decision, although it is defendants who may ultimately feel the force of judicial power, courts have, at least initially, more power over plaintiffs. To have any chance of attaining their ends, plaintiffs must comply with judicial requirements. In criminal cases, where the government appears as prosecutor, the judicial branch enjoys a relative advantage over the executive, and in *Burr* John Marshall made the most of it. The modern revolution in the rights of criminal defendants, beginning with *Mapp v. Ohio*,[81] was wrought by the Supreme Court drawing on its control over criminal procedure.

81. 367 U.S. 643 (1961).

Judicial power is generally greatest when drawing on the inherent strengths of the judicial institution. Control over the rules of procedure allowed Lord Mansfield to clear away some of the obstacles to the development of substantive rules of law.[82] Evidentiary presumptions can be utilized not only to facilitate decision making but also to induce litigants to behave as desired. Presuming a fact to be against a party's interest is the surest way of encouraging the party to produce evidence, if any, to the contrary.[83] Money damages are easier to order than specific performance, and where the remedy of specific performance is appropriate, it is easier to enforce inaction than to require affirmative acts.[84] Legal concepts such as title and debt are uniquely subject to legal control: title to property is clear, and debts are discharged if the appropriate court says so.[85] Ipse dixit.

Bare-bones judicial power is the power to resolve disputes. No more is required, and many of the world's courts, in fact, do nothing more. Common-law courts, however, have greatly magnified their power over the centuries by drawing on se-

82. HOLDSWORTH, *supra* note 10, at 493–494.

83. *See, e.g., Armory v. Delamirie,* 1 Strange 505, 93 Eng. Rep. 664 (K.B. 1722) (noting that in a case of trover for a jewel "the Chief Justice directed the jury, that unless the defendant did produce the jewel, and shew it not to be of the finest water, they should presume the strongest against him, and make the value of the best jewels the measure of their damages").

84. *See, e.g., Lumley v. Wagner,* 1 De G. M. & G. 604, 42 Eng. Rep. 687 (Ch. 1852) (ordering a singer, who wished to sing for one impresario in breach of her contract with another impresario, not to sing at all).

85. *See, e.g.,* ORTH, *supra* note 41, at 95–104.

cret sources. The rule of precedent made the judges legislators of a sort. To be effective, precedent requires records, and the common law engendered the world's first modern law reports. To increase the usefulness of the reports and the accompanying power of precedent, American courts perfected the form of judicial expression known as the opinion of the court, as opposed to the opinion of the various judges who constitute the court. By these simple devices, judicial power, as a practical matter, was vastly increased.

In addition, conscious of the judicial institution's inherent strengths as well as its inherent weaknesses—the one is as important as the other—astute judges have been able to exploit its latent power, while minimizing (or concealing) its defects. Control over procedure, rules of evidence, and remedies have been used to endow a relatively powerless branch of government with remarkable potency. An essentially disarmed institution, lacking the executive's power of the sword and the legislature's power of the purse, the judicial branch has had to discover its own sources of power: in reasoned argument, publicity, and the desire of a disputatious people for the peace it alone can provide.

3

Can the Common Law Be Unconstitutional?

C an a law be unconstitutional? The short answer, of course, is yes. Just as Thomas Babington Macaulay once observed that "every schoolboy knows who imprisoned Montezuma, and who strangled Atahualpa,"[1] so every American grade-schooler knows that courts in the United States can declare a law unconstitutional, and that unconstitutional means void and unenforceable. Yet Macaulay's well-informed schoolboy probably also knew that in England, the home of the common law, it was quite possible that a court would enforce an unconstitutional law—if by unconstitutional is meant something other and more than simply not adopted according to the constitutional process.

---

1. Thomas Babington Macaulay, *Lord Clive, in* 1 Critical and Historical Essays 479, 479 (1907). Montezuma, the Aztec ruler, was a captive of the Spanish under Hernán Cortés in 1520. Atahualpa, the last Inca ruler, was tried and executed on the orders of Francisco Pizarro in 1533.

Sir William Blackstone, the famous Commentator on the laws of England, had imagined—however uneasily—just such a case. "If the parliament will positively enact a thing to be done which is unreasonable," he said, "I know of no power that can control it."[2] Could a law authorize a judge to try all cases within his jurisdiction, Blackstone asked, including a case in which he himself is a party? Could a law, in other words, make a man a judge in his own case? Although he thought it a violation of natural law, "one of the evils civil government was intended to remedy,"[3] Blackstone also thought that the legislature could do it notwithstanding, and that English judges could do nothing about it. "If we could conceive it possible for the parliament to enact, that he should try as well his own causes as those of other persons, there is no court that has power to defeat the intention of the legislature, when couched in such evident and express words, as leave no doubt whether it was the intent of the legislature or no."[4] Power is the key. Although such an unreasonable and unjust statute would violate the (unwritten) English Constitution, it would be enforceable nonetheless. Any other result, Blackstone thought, would "set the judicial power above that

---

2. 1 WILLIAM BLACKSTONE, COMMENTARIES ON THE LAWS OF ENG-LAND 91 (1765) (hereinafter BL. COM.).

3. 4 BL. COM. 8 (1769).

4. 1 BL. COM. 91. The case of making a man a judge in his own case, which has intrigued jurists since the time of Littleton and Coke, is discussed more fully in JOHN V. ORTH, DUE PROCESS OF LAW, A BRIEF HISTORY 15–32 (2003).

of the legislature, which would be subversive of all government."[5] To his credit, the Commentator never conceded that such an outrageous act would be constitutional, only that English courts could not refuse to enforce it.

The unstated premise, then, of the American equation of the terms *unconstitutional* and *unenforceable* is the power—indeed, the duty—of American courts to refuse to enforce laws contrary to the (written) constitution. At least since the famous U.S. Supreme Court case of *Marbury v. Madison* in 1803, it has been settled doctrine in America that "a law repugnant to the constitution is void."[6] At the root of the reasoning in *Marbury* lies a simple syllogism: courts interpret the law; the Constitution is a law; therefore, courts interpret the Constitution. Interpreting the Constitution is no different, in other words, than interpreting a statute. But the Constitution is of higher authority than any statute; it declares itself the "supreme law of the land."[7] And unlike a statute, which may be repealed or qualified by a later statute—"an old statute gives place to a new one," as Blackstone conceded[8]—the Constitution is superior to all subsequent laws, except subsequent constitutional amendments. A constitution is a law, in other words, in the sense that the judicial branch interprets it, but not in the sense that the legislative branch

5. 1 BL. COM. 91.
6. 5 U.S. (1 Cranch) 137, 180 (1803). For further discussion of *Marbury*, see Essay 2.
7. U.S. CONST. art. VI, cl. 2.
8. 1 BL. COM. 89.

can repeal or modify it. In *Marbury* the Constitution, as judicially determined, did not permit the result intended by the legislature. The statute therefore could not be enforced, the American court, unlike its English counterpart, having the power to defeat it.

Whether necessarily convincing or not, the *Marbury* syllogism does serve to illustrate two meanings of the word *law*. A statute is a law, but so—at least in America—is the constitution. If the constitution is a law, can any part of it be unconstitutional? It seems hard to imagine with respect to the original text of the U.S. Constitution, which is without patent ambiguities or obvious internal contradictions, although its implicit recognition of slavery could raise questions under natural law.[9] A constitutional amendment, of course, may change the constitution, as the Twelfth Amendment changed the manner of choosing the president and vice president.[10] And one amendment may expressly repeal another, as the Twenty-first Amendment repealed the Prohibition Amendment.[11] Or a later amendment may qualify a prior amendment, as the Fourteenth Amendment, giving Congress power to enforce its provisions, impliedly conferred on federal courts power to decide cases against states that would

9. U.S. CONST. art. I, § 2, cl. 3 (representation of persons not free); *id.*, § 9, cl. 1 (importation of persons); *id.* art. IV, § 2, cl. 3 (fugitives from service or labor).

10. U.S. CONST. amend. XII, *superseding* art. II, § 1, cl. 3.

11. *Id.* amend. XXI, *repealing* amend. XVIII.

otherwise be barred by the Eleventh Amendment.[12] But a serious question would arise if a constitutional amendment attempted to deprive a state without its consent of equal representation in the U.S. Senate, the one thing the U.S. Constitution says even an amendment cannot do.[13]

In the multiconstitutioned United States, the question whether a constitution can be unconstitutional makes most sense when referring to state constitutions. The constitution of a state may violate the Constitution of the United States and be therefore unenforceable.[14] The North Carolina Constitution, for example, makes demonstration of the ability "to read and write any section of the Constitution in the English language"[15] a precondition for registering to vote, but this

12. *Id.* amend. XIV, § 5, *qualifying* amend. XI. *See* JOHN V. ORTH, THE JUDICIAL POWER OF THE UNITED STATES: THE ELEVENTH AMENDMENT IN AMERICAN HISTORY 127–135, 149 (1987).

13. U.S. CONST. art. V ("no State, without its Consent, shall be deprived of its equal Suffrage in the Senate"). Another entrenched clause, prohibiting amendments prior to 1808 concerning the importation of slaves or the imposition of a direct tax without apportionment, is now obsolete. Changing the basis of representation in the Senate might be possible if Article V were amended first, to remove the entrenched clause.

14. U.S. CONST. art. VI, cl. 2 ("This Constitution, and Laws of the United States which shall be made in Pursuance thereof; and all Treaties made, or which shall be made, under the Authority of the United States, shall be the supreme Law of the Land; and Judges in every State shall be bound thereby, any Thing in the Constitution or Laws of any State to the Contrary notwithstanding.").

15. N.C. CONST. art. VI, § 4. The literacy test first entered the North Carolina Constitution in 1900, part of an amendment that also included a

requirement has been held to violate the U.S. Constitution.[16] The same state constitution disqualifies from office "any person who shall deny the being of Almighty God,"[17] but this provision too has been held to violate the federal Constitution.[18] These provisions remain in the text of the state constitution; they simply cannot be enforced by any court, state or federal, and are therefore dead letters.

Although a constitution is a law, the more common meaning of the word is, of course, a statute. As Justice Joseph Story once put it when construing the words of the first Judiciary Act: "The laws of a state are more usually understood to mean the rules and enactments promulgated by the legislative authority thereof...."[19] Statutes certainly may—at least in America—be unconstitutional and unenforceable. Unconstitutionality does not prevent a statute from being

---

poll tax requirement and was intended to exclude African American voters, whose unequal educational opportunities and relative poverty made them less likely to qualify. *See* JOHN V. ORTH, THE NORTH CAROLINA STATE CONSTITUTION: A REFERENCE GUIDE 18, 135 (1993).

16. *Andrews v. Cody,* 327 F. Supp. 793 (M.D.N.C. 1971), *aff'd* 405 U.S. 1034 (1972); *Gaston County v. United States,* 395 U.S. 285 (1969).

17. N.C. CONST. art. VI, § 8. The religious test in its present form was first added to the North Carolina Constitution in 1868 by delegates to the state constitutional convention convinced that "no oath would bind a man who denied the existence of a higher power." *See* ORTH, *supra* note 15, at 137.

18. *Torcaso v. Watkins,* 367 U.S. 488 (1961).

19. *Swift v. Tyson,* 41 U.S. (16 Pet.) 1, 18 (1834). Story added to his definition of state laws "long established local customs having the force of laws."

adopted; it only prevents a court from enforcing it. Indeed, there is normally no way to determine if a statute is unconstitutional until a court, asked to enforce it, refuses to do so for that reason.[20] Until such determination, the statute is "on the books," presumptively valid. It even remains on the books after a determination of unconstitutionality, like the unconstitutional parts of the North Carolina Constitution, still there but of no effect. It is this reality that allows us to say that a "law" can be unconstitutional; it remains a law in some sense, albeit an empty one, since it is unenforceable.

But there is a third type of law, neither constitution nor statute: there is the common law. The common law, which originated in England in the twelfth century, was made over the years by the judges in their decisions of individual cases. These decisions not only resolved the disputes at issue, they also established rules for decision in other similar cases. Because of this origin, rules of the common law are often called case law, to distinguish them from statute law.[21]

20. A few state courts give advisory opinions concerning the constitutionality of a proposed law. *See, e.g.*, Opinions of the Justices to the Senate, 802 N.E.2d 565 (Mass. 2004) (a majority of justices advise that a bill limiting marriage to opposite-sex couples while providing civil unions with equal benefits for same-sex couples would violate the state constitution). For a comment on an earlier advisory opinion, see John V. Orth, *"Forever Separate and Distinct": Separation of Powers in North Carolina,* 62 N.C. L. REV. 1–28 (1983) (commenting on Advisory Opinion in re Separation of Powers, 295 S.E.2d 589 (1982)).

21. BLACK'S LAW DICT. 229 (case law), 1452 (statutory law) (8th ed. 2004).

The common law is far older than any written constitution, older even than any statute. One of the earliest statutes in the English law book, in fact, the statute De Donis Conditionalibus (1285), was enacted to overturn a line of common-law decisions concerning the effect of certain grants of land.[22] The common law was applied in the English colonies in North America and adopted one way or another by all American states after the Revolution[23]—except Louisiana, where French and Spanish influence allowed the civil law, derived originally from Roman law, to hold its own.[24] The U.S. Constitution presupposes the existence of the common law, using terms familiar from its vocabulary, such as ex post

22. 13 Edw. I, stat. 1, c. 1 (1285), 1 Stat. at Large 164 (William Hawkins ed. 1724). On the judicial decisions that led to the statute De Donis, the root of the fee tail, and its subsequent history, see John V. Orth, *Does the Fee Tail Exist in North Carolina?* 23 WAKE FOREST L. REV. 767, 773–778 (1988).

23. *See, e.g.,* N.C. Gen. Stat. § 4-1 ("All such parts of the common law as were heretofore in force and use within this State, or so much of the common law as is not destructive of, or repugnant to, or inconsistent with, the freedom and independence of this State and the form of government therein established, and which has not been otherwise provided for in whole or in part, not abrogated, repealed, or become obsolete, are hereby declared to be in full force within this State."). This statute, originally adopted in the colonial period, was reenacted in 1778 and has been interpreted to adopt the common law as it was on July 4, 1776. *Steelman v. City of New Bern,* 184 S.E.2d 239 (N.C. 1971).

24. Louisiana is today a mixed civil-law and common-law jurisdiction. *See generally* LOUISIANA: MICROCOSM OF A MIXED JURISDICTION (Vernon Valentine Palmer ed. 1999).

facto law,[25] bill of attainder,[26] and corruption of blood.[27] The Seventh Amendment in the Bill of Rights concerning the right to trial by jury simply incorporates by reference "the rules of the common law."[28]

Can any part of the common law be unconstitutional? The answer must, of course, be yes.[29] What cannot be done by a statute cannot be done by the common law. But this case is more complicated than the others because there is no determinate text of the common law, the reason it was traditionally called "unwritten law."[30] In fact, Justice Story, repeating the

25. U.S. Const. art. II, § 9, cl. 3 ("No Bill of attainder or ex post facto Law shall be passed.").

26. *Id.*

27. U.S. Const. art. III, § 3, cl. 2 ("no Attainder of Treason shall work Corruption of Blood").

28. Because the Seventh Amendment is interpreted to guarantee whatever right was accorded at ratification in 1791, *Markman v. Westview Instruments,* Inc., 517 U.S. 370 (1996), eighteenth-century English practice is of more than historical interest. *See* James Oldham, *The Seventh Amendment Right to Jury Trial: Late Eighteenth-Century Practice Reconsidered, in* Human Rights and Legal History: Essays in Honour of Brian Simpson 225–253 (Katherine O'Donovan & Gerry R. Rubin eds. 2000); Suja A. Thomas, *The Seventh Amendment, Modern Procedure, and the English Common Law,* 82 Wash. U. L. Q. 687 (2004).

29. *See, e.g., New York Times v. Sullivan,* 376 U.S. 254 (1964) (aspects of common law of libel as applied by state courts violate First Amendment); *Rosaro v. Blake,* 581 S.E.2d 41 (N.C. 2003) (questioning constitutionality of common-law presumption that illegitimate child is *filius nullius*).

30. *See* 1 Bl. Com. 63 ("The *lex non scripta,* or unwritten law, includes not only *general customs,* or the common law properly so called; but also the *particular customs* of certain parts of the kingdom; and likewise those

traditional view of the nature of the common law, actually denied that the rules declared by the courts were "laws" in the usual sense of that word: "In the ordinary use of language it will hardly be contended that the decisions of Courts constitute laws. They are, at most, only evidence of what the laws are; and are not of themselves laws. They are often reexamined, reversed, and qualified by the Courts themselves, whenever they are found to be either defective, or ill-founded, or otherwise incorrect."[31] While well grounded in history, Story's view was already losing its hold even as he spoke. The eventual triumph of positivism meant that judicial decisions are now generally regarded as laws. As Justice Oliver Wendell Holmes put it in the case that overturned Story's statutory construction, "[W]hether the law of the state shall be declared by its Legislature in a statute or by its highest court in a decision is not a matter of federal concern."[32]

The problem is that the American concept of unconstitutionality seems to presuppose the existence of written texts,

---

particular laws, that are by custom observed only in certain courts and jurisdictions.") (italics in original).

31. *Swift v. Tyson,* 41 U.S. (16 Pet.) 1, 18 (1834).

32. *Erie RR. v. Tompkins,* 304 U.S. 64, 78 (1938). Forty years earlier Holmes had explained that "the prophecies of what the courts will do in fact, and nothing more pretentious, are what I mean by the law." *The Path of the Law,* 10 HARV. L. REV. 457, 461 (1897). The "legal realist," Karl Llewellyn, went farther: "What officials do about disputes is to my mind the law itself." THE BRAMBLE BUSH 3 (1930)—a remark he later modified. *Id.* 8–9 (1951).

which is not surprising, since it developed as a way to resolve conflicts between written constitutions and statutes. In *The Federalist*, for example, Alexander Hamilton described judicial review solely in terms of conflicting texts: "A constitution is, in fact, and must be regarded by the judges as, a fundamental law. It therefore belongs to them to ascertain its meaning, as well as the meaning of any particular act proceeding from the legislative body. If there should happen to be an irreconcilable variance between the two, that which has the superior obligation and validity ought to be preferred; or, in other words, the Constitution ought to be preferred to the statute, the intention of the people to the intention of their agents."[33] The task of the judge exercising the power of judicial review has been graphically, if somewhat simplistically, described by one who actually did it as "to lay the article of the Constitution which is invoked beside the statute which is challenged and to decide whether the latter squares with the former."[34]

Avoiding conflicts between constitutions and the common law is a different matter. To take Blackstone's original example of a law making a man a judge in his own case, the Commentator had no doubt that any customary practice that produced such a result could not be recognized as part of the common law. "Customs must be *reasonable*,"[35] he said, and

33. THE FEDERALIST 492 (Benjamin Fletcher Wright ed. 1966).

34. *United States v. Butler*, 297 U.S. 1, 62 (1936) (Roberts, J.).

35. 1 BL. COM. 77 (italics in original). The Commentator added the characteristic qualification: "or rather, taken negatively, they must not be unreasonable."

legal authorities for hundreds of years had agreed that a custom that allowed a man to be his own judge would be "counter to reason."[36] While English judges lacked the power to defeat a statute, no matter how unreasonable, they did have the power to declare what the common law was, and they were convinced that it had to comport with reason. So high an authority as Sir Edward Coke was on record that "reason is the life of the law," "the common law itself is nothing else but reason,"[37] and Blackstone, generalizing, concluded that "what is not reason is not law."[38] By implication, then, the Commentator might have characterized an unreasonable statute as enforceable but not "law" in the true sense of the word. Of course, the presumption that the common law is impeccable is easier to maintain without an established text, gathered as it is from a mass of decisions that could be extended, distinguished, or even rejected. Until the reforms of legal reporting associated with Lord Mansfield in the latter half of the eighteenth century, it remained possible to dismiss the precedential value of many early cases by "doubting the reports."[39]

In America after the Revolution the judges continued to treat the common law as their peculiar domain. Not only did

36. THOMAS LITTLETON, ON TENURES § 212 (1481).

37. EDWARD COKE, COMMENTARY UPON LITTLETON § 138, p. 97b (1628). It was to this remark that Oliver Wendell Holmes made his famous riposte: "The life of the law has not been logic: it has been experience." THE COMMON LAW 5 (1881).

38. 1 BL. COM. 70.

39. For further discussion of law reports as "secret sources of judicial power," see Essay 2.

they decide what the constitution required and nullify statutes that violated it, they also made—and in some cases unmade—the common law.[40] "The common law of England," Justice Story had earlier written, "is not to be taken in all respects to be that of America."[41] And state courts agreed: "It cannot be necessary to cite cases to prove that those portions of the common law of England which are hostile to the spirit of our institutions, or which are not adapted to the existing state of things in this country, form no part of our law."[42]

As English courts progressively developed the common-law Rule against Perpetuities throughout the nineteenth century, American state courts generally followed suit,[43] although they retained the power to refuse to accept aspects of the rigorous Rule—as one court did to the consternation of Professor John Chipman Gray, the Rule's leading scholar, who thought it "a serious thing deliberately to break away from the consensus of the English-speaking world."[44] And

40. The reception statute may expressly exclude rules of the common law that are unconstitutional. *See, e.g.,* N.C. GEN. STAT. § 4-1 (receiving only "so much of the common law as is not destructive of, or repugnant to, or inconsistent with, the freedom and independence of this State and the form of government therein established").

41. *Van Ness v. Pacard,* 27 U.S. (2 Pet.) 137, 144 (1829).

42. *Parker v. Foote,* 19 Wend. 309 (N.Y. 1838) (Bronson, J.).

43. *See generally* JOHN CHIPMAN GRAY, THE RULE AGAINST PERPETUITIES (4th ed. by Roland Gray 1942).

44. *Id.* at Appendix G, § 869, p. 756, commenting on *Edgerly v. Barker,* 31 A. 900 (N.H. 1891) (reforming the grant to comply with the Rule rather than voiding it for violation of the Rule). *See also* JOHN REID, CHIEF JUSTICE: THE JUDICIAL WORLD OF CHARLES DOE 128–132 (1967).

Chief Justice Lemuel Shaw of Massachusetts early rejected the harsh English law on conspiracy as applied to labor organizations: "Although the common law in regard to conspiracy in this Commonwealth is in force, yet it will not necessarily follow that every indictment at common law for this offence is a precedent for a similar indictment in this State."[45] But judicial acceptance or refusal of some rule or other of the common law has not generally been understood as either legislation, the prerogative of another branch of government, or judicial review in the usual sense; rather, it has been thought of as the more or less routine work of a common-law court. As Chief Justice John Marshall put it in *Marbury*, "It is emphatically the duty of the judicial department to say what the law is."[46]

The judges made the common law, but the legislature has since the beginning been able to undo it. "Where the common law and a statute differ," Blackstone long ago conceded, "the common law gives place to the statute."[47] Can a statute that alters a rule of the common law ever violate the constitution? The question might arise under the takings clause, prohibiting the taking of private property "for public use" without "just compensation."[48] Because so much property

45. *Comm. v. Hunt*, 45 Mass. (4 Metc.) 111 (1842). *See also* JOHN V. ORTH, COMBINATION AND CONSPIRACY: A LEGAL HISTORY OF TRADE UNIONISM 95 (1991).

46. 5 U.S. (1 Cranch) at 177.

47. 1 BL. COM. 89.

48. U.S. CONST. amend. V (applying to acts of federal government). The takings clause is applied to the states through the due process clause

law, and therefore the title to so much property, depends on the common law, a statute altering one of its rules may indeed be unconstitutional. If what is taken is a fee simple, the result is obvious, but in many cases the taking involves an interest less than a fee, and in such cases it is at least arguable that what is taken is not property in the common-law sense. This is especially true of so-called regulatory takings, that is, government regulations that restrict the use of property, taking away one or more of the legal rights of the owner.

It is also possible, even in cases in which all uses are taken, that a court may find that the common law, properly understood, had not recognized the right after all. Although it had been oft-repeated common-law dogma that the ownership of land extended upward from the surface "to an indefinite extent" (as Blackstone said),[49] "even up to heaven" (in the words of Sir Edward Coke),[50] when the needs of modern air travel led Congress to declare the "navigable air space" to be a public highway, the U.S. Supreme Court found no taking of private property. Exclusive control by the surface owner

---

of the Fourteenth Amendment. *Chicago, Burlington & Quincy RR. v. Chicago,* 166 U.S. 226 (1897). All state constitutions except North Carolina's now include a Takings Clause, 1 PHILIP NICHOLS, THE LAW OF EMINENT DOMAIN § 1.3, at 1–95 (3d ed. 2004). In North Carolina the law-of-the-land clause, N.C. CONST. art I, § 19, performs the same function. *See* ORTH, *supra* note 15, at 58.

49. 2 BL. COM. 18.

50. COKE, *supra* note 37, at § 1, p. 4a (Coke's translation of the final phrase in the common-law maxim *cujus est solum ejus est usque ad coelum*). For a science fiction story capitalizing on the common-law position, see ROBERT A. HEINLEIN, THE MAN WHO SOLD THE MOON (1950).

extends upward only as far as "the immediate reaches of the enveloping atmosphere." "The landowner owns at least as much of the space above the ground as he can occupy or use in connection with the land,"[51] the Supreme Court said, but no more. The common law, it turned out, was not exactly what the sages had said it was.

Although traditional common-law judges are far more likely to add rules than to subtract them,[52] more activist American judges, confronted by situations unknown to earlier ages, show less reluctance. Can the abrogation of a common-law rule by common-law decision rather than by legislation be an unconstitutional taking? Although a state has received the common law by statute,[53] courts have been known later to reject undoubted aspects of it as it was at the time of reception. The difficulty is determining the operative moment of rejection: Was the common law received as it then was, and later changed?—in which case a right would seem to have been taken. Or was the rule in question

---

51. *United States v. Causby*, 328 U.S. 256, 264 (1946). *See generally* JOHN SCURLOCK, RETROACTIVE LEGISLATION AFFECTING INTERESTS IN LAND (1953).

52. For a description of the substantive consequences of the common law's ability to "add but not subtract," see John V. Orth, *The Mystery of the Rule in Shelley's Case*, 7 GREEN BAG 2D 45 (2003).

53. In addition to general reception statutes, there may be special statutes directing the adoption of specific parts of the common law. *See, e.g.,* Title 60 Oregon Stat. 2001 § 299.1 ("the common law of powers [of appointment] is hereby declared to be the law in this state, except as modified by statute").

never received at all?—in which case there was no right to be taken in the first place, a fact that became apparent only much later.[54]

Judges traditionally defer to the legislature to reform the common law of property, in part because of the argument that change would unsettle titles, in part because of the doctrine of separation of powers. While legislation normally applies only prospectively, change of the common law has traditionally affected prior as well as subsequent transactions.[55] The theory of the common law, that what the judges only lately recognized had always been the law, avoided the appearance (if not the reality) of retrospective application. Not only would changing the rules unsettle titles, change by the judges would resemble legislation. As one judge reluctantly enforcing the archaic Rule in Shelley's Case put it: "Repeal is the duty of the legislative branch of our government, and the judiciary cannot legislate by refusing to follow the Rule."[56]

54. See *Abo Petroleum Corp. v. Amstutz*, 600 P.2d 278 (N.M. 1979) (construing state's common-law reception statute and declining to apply common-law doctrine of destructibility of contingent remainders), *noted in* 10 N. Mex. L. Rev. 471 (1980); *Johnson v. Amstutz*, 678 P.2d 1169, 1170 (N.M. 1984) (holding that "the doctrine is not now and *has never been* the law of New Mexico") (italics added).

55. Courts have begun to apply new rules only prospectively. *See, e.g., Sullivan v. Burkin*, 460 N.E.2d 571 (Mass. 1984) (concerning property subject to spouse's elective share).

56. *Sybert v. Sybert*, 254 S.W.2d 999, 1002 (Tex. 1953) (Griffin, J., concurring). When Texas finally abandoned the venerable Rule, it did so by legislation. Tex. Civ. Stat. art. 1291a (1964). Restatement (Second) of

Obviously, the most difficult case would involve a change in a common-law rule that had previously been recognized by courts in the jurisdiction. The recent Restatement of Servitudes, for example, would allow the relocation of easements by burdened landowners without the consent of the easement owners.[57] Although it is admitted that the "weight of authority in the United States" is to the contrary,[58] the Restatement adopts "the civil law rule that is in effect in Louisiana and a few other states."[59] Found in the Louisiana Civil Code,[60] the rule in question was adopted by the Louisiana legislature and can be changed only by the legislature, and then only prospectively.[61]

Despite its resemblance to a code, the Restatement is no more than a statement (or restatement) of the common law, available as a source of law to common-law judges in their

---

PROPERTY: DONATIVE TRANSFERS § 30.1 (3) recommends that the Rule in Shelley's Case should be abolished prospectively, whether by statute or judicial decision.

57. RESTATEMENT (THIRD) OF PROPERTY: SERVITUDES § 4.8(3) (2000). *Compare* Susan French, *Relocating Easements: Restatement (Third): Servitudes § 4.8(3)*, 38 REAL PROP. PROB. & TR. J. 1 (2003), *with* John V. Orth, *Relocating Easements: A Response to Professor French, id.* 645 (2004).

58. RESTATEMENT: (THIRD) OF PROPERTY: SERVITUDES § 4.8 Reporter's Note, at 578 (2000). Many authorities, old and new, deny the burdened landowner's right to relocate unilaterally without the easement owner's consent. *See, e.g.,* JON W. BRUCE & JAMES W. ELY JR., THE LAW OF EASEMENTS AND LICENSES IN LAND § 7:13, at 7–26 (2001).

59. RESTATEMENT: (THIRD) OF PROPERTY: SERVITUDES § 4.8 cmt. f, p. 563 (2000). *See also id.* Reporter's Note, at 575.

60. La. Civ. Code art. 748. *See also id.* art. 695.

61. *Id.* art. 6.

decisions of individual cases.[62] If its new rule were applied to existing easements by statute, it could be held an unconstitutional taking.[63] But the common-law way of doing things conceals, perhaps even from the judges, the reality of what they are doing. In spirit the common law is preconstitutional, in the sense of preceding all written constitutions and modern forms of government. Even after more than 200 years under written constitutions and a rising tide of positivism, American judges can still think of their decisions, as Justice Story did, as not laws but "at most" only evidence of what the laws are—susceptible to be revised, reversed, and qualified in the light of changing notions of reason or utility.[64] Only recently have scholars and judges begun to consider the possibility that takings wrought by changes in the common law rather than legislation might also violate the constitution.[65]

In a world of texts, the common law is not a text but a process.[66] When written constitutions were added to the

62. *See M.P.M. Builders v. Dwyer*, 809 N.E.2d 1053 (Mass. 2004) (adopting Restatement rule concerning relocation of easements and applying it to preexisting easements despite recognition that state law previously did not permit relocation without consent).

63. The issues would be (1) whether the taking was "for public use," and (2) whether "just compensation" in the form of the substitute easement was adequate.

64. *See* note 31, *supra*.

65. *See, e.g., Stevens v. Cannon Beach*, 510 U.S. 1207 (1994) (Scalia, J., dissenting from denial of certiorari). *See generally* Barton H. Thompson Jr., *Judicial Takings*, 76 VA. L. REV. 1449 (1990).

66. I am aware of the current debate, associated with Stanley Fish's book IS THERE A TEXT IN THIS CLASS? (1980), about whether there is

common-law tradition—or, more precisely, when written constitutions entered the common-law tradition—it was without conscious recognition of the dynamic thereby established. No sooner was the constitution reduced to writing than it became subject to the common-law process. The meanings of constitutional guarantees are developed, like statutes and the rules of the common law itself, from case to case.[67] As the judges develop the law of the constitution, they occasionally recognize a conflict with a traditional rule or practice of the common law. In case of obvious conflict, the rule must inevitably fall. Although the primacy accorded to reason both in interpreting the constitutions and in developing the common law reduces the risk of conflict between the two, and although the common law, notoriously malleable in the hands of adroit judges, normally proceeds by distinguishing rather than reversing prior case law, the courts cannot enforce a law, even a rule of the common law, contrary to the constitution. The final irony may be that, while a law—including a rule of the common law—can be unconstitutional, whatever freedom the judges lost in developing the common law (and it was not very much) was more than compensated by their gain in the freedom to develop the law of the constitution.

(or can be) a distinction between text and process. Suffice it to say, I think there can be, although I recognize, now more clearly than before, that the distinction is not so sharp as once thought.

67. For a "case history" of constitutional development by common-law methods, *see* ORTH, *supra* note 4.

4

The Persistence of the Common Law

It is generally understood that the origins of the common law are to be found in the reign of King Henry II in the twelfth century. No very great knowledge of medieval history is required to say that the conditions of society then were very different than they are now. The conquest of England by the Normans under Henry's great-grandfather Duke William of Normandy was barely a century in the past, and its consequences were far from exhausted. The French language continued to be spoken by the ruling elite and would remain the language of English law for centuries to come.[1] The king held title to all the land in England, either in demesne or

---

1. The first book on English property law was written in (a form of) French. THOMAS LITTLETON, TENURES (1481). As translated and annotated by Sir Edward Coke more than a century later, it became the foundation of English and American property law. EDWARD COKE, THE FIRST PART OF THE INSTITUTES OF THE LAWS OF ENGLAND; OR, A COMMENTARY ON LITTLETON (1628).

through vassals. More than a system of landholding, feudalism was also a way of organizing society militarily, economically, and politically. Technological limitations bounded material society on every side; it was truly "a world lit only by fire."[2] Intellectual life was concentrated in the church, which monopolized all learning not purely practical. However difficult it is to recapture in the imagination the physical reality of the Middle Ages, even more elusive is its mentality.

There is no need to describe by contrast the modern world in which we all live and work; differences from the medieval world confront us at every turn. In the early twenty-first century our society has little in common with that of the late twelfth century—except the common law. Yet law, we are often told, is a product of society, an effect not a cause, superstructure not foundation. Nonetheless, the common law that originated so long ago is with us yet. In what sense, we may ask, do the twelfth and the twenty-first centuries—and all the centuries in between—share the same legal system? To answer that question, we must first unbundle that complex and durable social construct, the common law. More than a mere body of rules, the common law was also a set of institutions and a certain way of doing things.

The purely institutional answer to the question of what there is in common over all the centuries of common-law history is a system of courts to resolve disputes. All legal sys-

2. Use of this phrase from the title of William Manchester's book on "the medieval mind and the Renaissance" (1992) does not signify acceptance of everything contained therein.

tems have courts, but the distinguishing feature of the common law is the priority of the courts over the rules. This is a point to be insisted upon because it strikes most people today as getting the story backward. A legal system, modern people would expect, should begin with rules and then proceed to the establishment of the institutions that enforce them. Rules about rights and duties would seem to be of the essence; everything else in the legal system, while important, would appear to be secondary. That thoroughly modern thinker, Jeremy Bentham, captured the idea when he coined the phrase "adjective law" to describe the rules concerning jurisdiction, procedure, evidence, and so forth.[3] The rules of substantive law, the rules about rights and duties, are the nouns and verbs; the rest are mere modifiers. However logical, Bentham was no historian. The common law began not with rules but with courts.

Sir Frederick Pollock and Frederic William Maitland, the preeminent historians of the early common law, describe the reign of Henry II as being "of supreme importance in the history of our law," but, they continue, "it was rather as an organizer and governor than as a legislator that Henry was active."[4] Unlike Hammurabi, Justinian, and Napoleon, King

3. *See* JEREMY BENTHAM, PRINCIPLES OF JUDICIAL PROCEDURE, *in* 2 WORKS OF JEREMY BENTHAM 6 (J. Bowring ed. 1838–1843). *See also* GERALD J. POSTEMA, BENTHAM AND THE COMMON LAW TRADITION 342–344 (1986).

4. 1 FREDERICK POLLOCK & FREDERIC WILLIAM MAITLAND, THE HISTORY OF ENGLISH LAW BEFORE THE TIME OF EDWARD I, at 136 (2d ed. 1898).

Henry gave his name to no code. Pollock and Maitland even doubt whether the king established "any one new rule which we should call a rule of substantive law." Instead, they say, he was "for ever busy with new devices for enforcing the law."[5] Edward I, whose accession in 1272 marks the end of Pollock and Maitland's *History of English Law*, was a lawgiver, called in fact "the English Justinian,"[6] but he too left his mark not with an imperial code but with a series of landmark statutes, mainly concerned with property law, like De Donis Conditionalibus (1285),[7] the root of the fee tail, and Quia Emptores (1290),[8] the basis for free alienation of land. Unlike other of the world's legal systems, the common law was founded without a great burst of legislation. Yet it has endured as well as, if not better than, other legal systems and has spread with English settlers around the world. The fact of the matter is that courts and "devices for enforcing the law" wear better than rules. A great "organizer and governor" rivals or excels a great legislator.

---

5. *Id.* at 136.

6. E. COBHAM BREWER, THE DICTIONARY OF PHRASE AND FABLE 694 (1894) (s.v. Justinian). *See generally* T.F.T. PLUCKNETT, LEGISLATION OF EDWARD I (1949).

7. 13 Edw. I, c. 1 (1285). The statute De Donis, one of the earliest English statutes, was enacted to overturn a line of common-law decisions, the source of the fee simple conditional. For its background and subsequent history, see John V. Orth, *Does the Fee Tail Exist in North Carolina?* 23 WAKE FOREST L. REV. 767, 773–778 (1988).

8. 18 Edw. I (1290).

Rules risk impermanence because they must be formulated to answer the questions put to them at the time. At the beginning of the twentieth century, a great English law professor observed: "No one can seriously imagine that the Common Law of 600 years ago would have an intelligible answer to many of the legal questions of modern life. We know, as a matter of fact, that it answered some questions in the opposite sense to that in which we now answer them, e.g. a simple executory contract had no legal effect then."[9] And in America about the same time Professor John Chipman Gray ridiculed the notion of a sort of latent law only awaiting discovery by the judges when he asked: "What was the Law in the time of Richard Coeur de Lion on the liability of a telegraph company to the persons to whom a message is sent?"[10] The absence of telegraph law in the days before the telegraph should come as no surprise—any more than its obsolescence today in the Internet age. Nor should the backwardness of the common law in commercial cases surprise us. The world had not yet undergone the commercial revolution, let alone the industrial one, when the common law began.

9. W. M. GELDART, INTRODUCTION TO ENGLISH LAW 9 (9th ed. by D.C.M. Yardley 1984) (1st ed. entitled ELEMENTS OF ENGLISH LAW 1911). On the enforceability of executory contracts Professor P. S. Atiyah thinks it may be time to return to the original common-law position. THE RISE AND FALL OF FREEDOM OF CONTRACT 754–764 (1979).

10. JOHN CHIPMAN GRAY, THE NATURE AND SOURCES OF THE LAW 99 (2d ed. by Roland Gray 1927) (1st ed. 1909).

Not that rules can be safely ignored in telling the story of the common law's uncommon persistence; particularly is this true of land law, where the common law's development was precocious.[11] The fee simple and the life estate may have arisen in the days of feudalism, but they remain the basic building blocks of modern property law, having spread from real to personal property, particularly through the law of trusts.[12] The joint tenancy with its associated right of survivorship dates from the thirteenth century,[13] but it has survived into modern times and been adapted to forms of property, such as bank and brokerage accounts, unknown to the Middle Ages. Of course, the line of development from then to now has not been straight. The right of survivorship, while it may have originated in the need of the feudal system to fix liability for feudal dues, early showed its worth in the use of trusts to defeat the collection of those very dues. And it fell from favor generally, but never disappeared, when sole

---

11. *See* S.F.C. MILSOM, A NATURAL HISTORY OF THE COMMON LAW 53 (2003); 2 WILLIAM HOLDSWORTH, HISTORY OF ENGLISH LAW 355 (4th ed. 1936).

12. In England, the land of its birth, the legal life estate was abolished by the Law of Property (Amendment) Act (1924), 15 & 16 Geo. V, c. 5. Life estates (and all future interests) in that country exist today only as equitable interests. In America the legal life estate is still with us, although sophisticated property lawyers recommend against its creation. *See* JESSE DUKEMINIER & STANLEY M. JOHANSON, WILLS, TRUSTS, AND ESTATES 562–66 (6th ed. 2000).

13. Anne L. Spitzer, *Joint Tenancy with Right of Survivorship: A Legacy from Thirteenth Century England,* 16 TEX. TECH. L. REV. 629 (1985).

ownership of property was preferred in the nineteenth century. Today the expense and delay of probate have led to its widespread revival.[14]

Likewise the tenancy by the entirety, an estate reserved to married persons,[15] which also incorporates the valuable right of survivorship, began in the Middle Ages when the concept of marriage as the union of a man and a woman was taken to its logical conclusion, that the married couple held the land as one owner, not as two co-owners.[16] The management of the property, of course, in keeping with medieval preconceptions, was left to the man: "Husband and wife were one, and the husband was the one."[17] The old conception that the married couple becomes one person in law continues to find expression in the modern rule that no interest in property

14. *See* John V. Orth, *Joint Tenancy Law*, Plus ca Change…, 5 GREEN BAG 2D 173 (2002); John V. Orth, *The Joint Tenancy Makes a Comeback in North Carolina*, 69 N.C. L. REV. 491 (1991).

15. As pressure to recognize same-sex couples has built, two states have made tenancies by the entirety available to couples ineligible to marry under state law. Haw. Rev. Stat. § 509.2 (reciprocal beneficiaries); 15 Vt. Stat. Ann. tit. 23, § 1204 (civil unions). *See* John V. Orth, *Night Thoughts: Reflections on the Debate Concerning Same-Sex Marriage*, 3 NEV. L. J. 560–71 (2003). In Massachusetts, by judicial decision, same-sex couples are allowed to marry and are therefore eligible for all the legal incidents of marriage, including the ability to take title to property as tenants by the entirety.

16. *See* John V. Orth, *Tenancy by the Entirety: The Strange Career of the Common Law Marital Estate*, 1997 B.Y.U. L. REV. 35, 38–39.

17. JOHN E. CRIBBET ET AL., CASES AND MATERIALS ON PROPERTY 317 (8th ed. 2002). *See also* Elizabeth Cady Stanton, *On Divorce* (1861) (attributing remark to Blackstone), *in* 2 MAN CANNOT SPEAK FOR HER: KEY TEXTS OF THE EARLY FEMINISTS 236, 237 (Karlyn Kohrs Campbell ed. 1989).

held in tenancy by the entirety can be transferred by either spouse acting alone; both must join in the conveyance. And in many states a creditor of one spouse cannot levy on property held in tenancy by the entirety, only a creditor of both.[18] Today, after male domination has succumbed to the modern recognition of a married woman's legal personality, the tenancy remains the preferred form of landownership for married couples in states still recognizing it.[19]

The story with respect to the rules of contract and tort is more complicated. Although problems that would today be pigeonholed in those categories arose repeatedly over the long history of the common law, they attracted less attention than property problems because until modern times almost all of society's wealth was tied up in land—and because, or perhaps in consequence, the common law long resolved such questions by complicated procedural devices that obscured the real issues.[20] When in the eighteenth and nineteenth centuries rules concerning contract and tort did at last begin to emerge from the shadows, they inevitably reflected the individualistic theories of the time, which explains how the common law with its origins in the days of feudal-

---

18. *See* Orth, *supra* note 16, at 35, 40.

19. *See* John V. Orth, *Tenancies by the Entirety, in* 4 Thompson on Real Property § 33.06, pp. 126–127 (2d Thomas ed. 2004). In England tenancies by the entirety were abolished by the Law of Property Act (1925), 15 & 16 Geo. V, c. 20 § 39(6), sch. 1, and the estates converted into joint tenancies.

20. *See* Milsom, *supra* note 11, at 25–50.

ism can seemingly incorporate rules reflective of classical economics.[21]

The force of tradition has kept many rules of the common law green, sometimes long after the conditions that fostered them have passed away.[22] Truly harmful rules have been eliminated by legislation or judicial initiative. Sometimes new rules have been recognized to bypass troublesome old ones. The resulting complexity may have contributed to the apparent majesty of the law; it certainly augmented the income of lawyers needed to operate the system! In the United States the doctrine of separation of powers inhibited (but not too much) the judicial willingness to innovate. Where the courts have failed to keep pace with social developments, it has become necessary to enact statutes to bring about needed changes; indeed, in recent years statutes have superseded (or simply codified) many of the substantive rules of the common law.

But the triumph of statute has been more apparent than real. Legislation affecting the common law has often been the initiative of lawyers in the legislature or the academy. The adoption of the first installment of the modern statutory reform of English land law, the Real Property Acts (1833), as described by Lord Campbell, one of its sponsors, was hardly

21. For further thoughts on the "ideology of the common law," see Essay 5.

22. For an example, see John V. Orth, *The Mystery of the Rule in Shelley's Case,* 7 GREEN BAG 2D 45 (2003).

a model of deliberative lawmaking: "They quietly passed through both Houses of Parliament without one single syllable being altered in any of them. This is the only wise way of legislating on such a subject. They had been drawn by the Real Property Commissioners, printed and extensively circulated, and repeatedly revised, with the advantage of the observations of skilful men studying them in their closet. A mixed and numerous deliberative assembly is wholly unfit for such work."[23] Much the same may said of the passage through modern American legislatures of the various Uniform Acts, laborious products of the National Conference of Commissioners on Uniform State Laws.

And the courts have approached the statutes in a typically common-law way. Although the day may be past when judges routinely discount the significance of statutes by saying that they merely restate the common law, courts continue to treat statutes in ways similar to their treatment of common-law precedents. This is obviously true of loosely worded statutes such as the English Statute of Frauds (1677), reenacted in one form or another in all American jurisdictions, and subject in both countries to seemingly endless litigation.[24] In America, too, the Sherman Act (1890)—"Every contract, com-

23. 2 Life of John, Lord Campbell 29 (2d ed. by his daughter Mrs. Hardcastle 1881).

24. 29 Car. II, c. 3 (1677). *See* Caroline N. Brown, Statute of Frauds, 4 Corbin on Contracts § 12.4, p. 18 (Joseph M. Perillo ed. 1997); 2 James Kent, Commentaries on American Law 511 note d (12th ed. by O. W. Holmes 1873); Milsom, *supra* note 11, at 26.

bination..., or conspiracy, in restraint of trade...is hereby declared to be illegal"[25]—was little more than a legislative directive to the courts to create a comprehensive body of antitrust law. Likewise in the mid–twentieth century, federal courts found in the statute conferring on them jurisdiction to hear labor cases authority to create a body of law for the enforcement of collective bargaining agreements.[26]

The same is also, if more subtly, true of much more detailed legislation. Common-law judges do not customarily begin their reasoning with the words of a statute, as judges in the world's civil law systems are expected to do.[27] Instead, a statute is characteristically approached through prior cases that applied it. If none exists, judges refer to other similar statutes that have been the subject of judicial decision, or rehearse at length the conditions that led to its adoption and something of its legislative history—subjects outside the ordinary purview of civil law judges.[28] John Chipman Gray, with characteristic directness, even denied that statutes are law at all, only "sources of law" until applied by a court.[29]

The common law, as already mentioned, was prior to all statutes: courts were created before the first parliament was

---

25. Act of July 2, 1890, ch. 647, 26 Stat. 209.

26. *Textile Workers of America v. Lincoln Mills of Alabama*, 353 U.S. 448 (1957).

27. *See* ALAN WATSON, THE MAKING OF THE CIVIL LAW 168 (1981).

28. *See* J. M. KELLY, A SHORT HISTORY OF WESTERN LEGAL THEORY 312 (1992).

29. GRAY, *supra* note 10, at 152–155.

summoned.[30] And while the supremacy of statutes over the common law is firmly established—"Where the common law and a statute differ," Blackstone conceded, "the common law gives place to the statute"[31]—the fact of the common law's presence has been of major significance. For one thing, it allows a distracted legislature to leave whole areas to common-law ordering. Describing Virginia's legislative program after the American Revolution, Thomas Jefferson reported that "the common law of England, by which is meant, that part of the English law which was anterior to the date of the oldest statutes extant, is made the basis of the work."[32] No attempt was made to enact it in code form; it was, Jefferson said, "to be collected from the usual monuments of it." All that was needed was to make a few "necessary alterations"—such as abolishing primogeniture and establishing religious freedom—and to reenact "so much of the whole body of the British statutes, and of acts of [the colonial] assembly, as were thought proper to be retained."[33]

30. *See* Bryce Lyon, A Constitutional and Legal History of Medieval England 413 (1960).

31. 1 William Blackstone, Commentaries on the Laws of England 89 (1765).

32. Thomas Jefferson, Notes on the State of Virginia 137 (William Peden ed. 1954) (first published 1787). Jefferson here succumbed to the myth of the extreme antiquity of the common law.

33. *Id.* On the general question of the continued effectiveness of British statutes in America after the Revolution, see Elizabeth Gaspar Brown, British Statutes in American Law, 1776–1836 (1964).

The pervasiveness of the common law has left its mark on American law to this day. The resolution of legal issues still governed by essentially common-law rules—for example, questions of legal capacity, undue influence, fraud, and duress in the formation of legal relationships—exhibits a commonality lacking in areas governed by state legislation. Because of its traditional emphasis on biological kinship, the common law did not recognize the legal adoption of children. Statutes are required. As a result, the consequences of adoption vary widely from state to state. On the rights of a surviving spouse to a share of a decedent's estate—handled inadequately by the common-law rights of dower and curtesy and now superseded almost everywhere by statute—the authors of a leading casebook post a conspicuous warning: "*Caution.* There is no subject in this book on which there is more statutory variation than the surviving spouse's elective share."[34]

Where the common law persisted, not only did it lull the legislature into inactivity, it also dulled its mind when it did legislate. Standards of statutory drafting in common-law systems were (and sometimes still are) surprisingly lax, a laxity made tolerable by the possibility of judicial remediation. Yet at the same time, statutes in common-law systems are occasionally extremely detailed, to the consternation of lawyers trained in civil law systems.[35] Operating against the backdrop

34. *See* DUKEMINIER & JOHANSON, *supra* note 12, at 480.
35. *See* E. ALLAN FARNSWORTH, AN INTRODUCTION TO THE LEGAL SYSTEM OF THE UNITED STATES 73 (3d ed. 1996). Professor Farnsworth

of the common law, a statute may be functionally no more than an amendment to existing law and therefore apparently too simple, yet if the legislature fears restrictive judicial interpretation, it may be made correspondingly complex.

The common law and the statutes interact in complicated ways, the one sometimes stimulating the development of the other.[36] The legislative adoption of the Uniform Commercial Code with its implied warranty of merchantability in the sale of goods inspired recognition in some jurisdictions of a common-law warranty of habitability in residential leases, which inspired in turn legislation on the subject in still other jurisdictions.[37] And the warranty of habitability, whether common law or statutory, contributed to the growing liability of landlords for injuries to tenants.[38] Uniform acts often cover less than the whole field, creating an additional layer of complexity. The Uniform Commercial Code, for example,

---

lists other causes of the greater complexity of statutes in common-law, as opposed to civil-law, systems: "a pluralistic society, a highly developed economy, and a federal system," as well as "the lower level of abstraction on which the common law lawyer operates" and "pressures of the enactment process [that] often narrow the scope of legislation." *Id.*

36. For an account of the interaction between statute and common law in the history of labor law, see JOHN V. ORTH, COMBINATION AND CONSPIRACY: A LEGAL HISTORY OF TRADE UNIONISM, 1721–1906, at 25–42 (1991).

37. *See* John V. Orth, *Sale of Defective Houses: Cicero and the Moral Choice,* 6 GREEN BAG 2D 163 (2003).

38. *See, e.g., Sargeant v. Ross,* 308 A.2d 528 (1973). *See also* ROBERT S. SCHOSHINSKI, AMERICAN LAW OF LANDLORD AND TENANT § 4: 9, pp. 204–206 (1980).

applies only to transactions involving merchants, leaving a residual category of common-law ordering for private transactions.[39]

Although statutes are today what most people think of as laws, constitutions are what most Americans think of as the law nonpareil. In theory, one might have expected the advent of written constitutions to break the continuity of common-law history. In the words of one eighteenth-century judge who had served both the royal and the republican governments: "At the time of our separation from Great Britain, we were thrown into a similar situation with a set of people shipwrecked and cast on a marooned island—without laws, without magistrates, without government, or any legal authority."[40] Returned to the state of nature, Americans looked back to the source of the common law across the seeming gulf of the Revolution. But unlike later French, Russian, or Chinese revolutionaries, the Americans did not make the break with the past an opportunity to forge a new legal code. The common law bridged the gap without apparent effort, or even much apparent thought—except as to the question of a federal common law of crime.[41]

39. *See, e.g., Porter v. Wertz,* 416 N.Y.S.2d 254, *aff'd* 421 N.E.2d 500 (1981) (distinguishing "statutory estoppel" under the Uniform Commercial Code from "equitable estoppel" at common law).

40. *Bayard v. Singleton,* 1 N.C. 5 (1787) (Ashe, J.).

41. *See Symposium: Federal Common Law of Crime,* 4 LAW & HIST. REV. 223 (1986).

It is tempting to conclude that the common law survived in America for the same reason the English language did, because there was no practical alternative. Indeed, Chancellor Kent defended the post-Revolutionary citation of English cases by arguing that "the dignity or independence of our Courts is no more affected by adopting these decisions, than in adopting the English language."[42] But history has shown that law is more easily shed than language. The French continued to speak *la belle langue* even as they changed the currency, weights and measures, and the calendar—and adopted the Code Napoleon. On the other hand, the Norman conquerors centuries earlier were ceasing to speak French even as they made English law.

Written constitutions might also have threatened the common-law tradition in another way. A written constitution is a sort of code, and codes generate a characteristic (and non-common-law) jurisprudential approach. But constitutions too have been given the common-law treatment.[43] In part this was inevitable (and presumably intended), given the use of compendious and inherently common-law terms. The text of the U.S. Constitution forbids without explanation or definition ex post facto laws,[44] bills of attainder,[45] and corrup-

---

42. *Manning v. Manning,* 1 Johns. Ch. 527, 531 (N.Y. 1815).

43. *See* David A. Strauss, *Common Law Constitutional Interpretation,* 62 U. Chi. L. Rev. 131 (1995).

44. U.S. Const. art. II, § 9, cl. 3 ("No Bill of attainder or ex post facto Law shall be passed.").

45. *Id.*

tion of blood.[46] And the Seventh Amendment, guaranteeing
the right to trial by jury in civil cases, simply incorporates
by reference "the rules of the common law."[47] "Due process
of law," guaranteed by state and federal constitutions alike,
is hardly self-explanatory, and the connection between procedural abuses and, say, the "due process" right of couples to
practice birth control,[48] of a woman to choose an abortion,[49]
of consenting adults to engage in sodomy,[50] or of same-sex
couples to marry[51] is not obvious and must be found by a
close reading of a long series of decided cases.

46. U.S. CONST. art. III, § 3, cl. 2 ("no Attainder of Treason shall work
Corruption of Blood").

47. U.S. CONST. amend. VII. Because the Seventh Amendment is in-
terpreted by the U.S. Supreme Court to guarantee whatever right was
accorded at ratification in 1791, *Markman v. Westview Instruments, Inc.*, 517
U.S. 370 (1996), eighteenth-century English practice is of more than his-
torical interest. *See* James Oldham, *The Seventh Amendment Right to Jury
Trial: Late Eighteenth-Century Practice Reconsidered, in* HUMAN RIGHTS
AND LEGAL HISTORY: ESSAYS IN HONOUR OF BRIAN SIMPSON 225–253
(Katherine O'Donovan & Gerry R. Rubin eds. 2000); Suja A. Thomas,
The Seventh Amendment, Modern Procedure and the English Common Law,
82 WASH. U. L. Q. 687 (2004).

48. *Griswold v. Connecticut,* 381 U.S. 479 (1965) (married couples); *Eisen-
stadt v. Baird,* 405 U.S. 438 (1972) (unmarried couples).

49. *Roe v. Wade,* 410 U.S. 113 (1973). For the context, see JOHN V. ORTH,
DUE PROCESS OF LAW: A BRIEF HISTORY 75–80 (2003).

50. *Lawrence v. Texas,* 529 U.S. 558 (2003).

51. *Goodridge v. Department of Public Health,* 798 N.E.2d 941 (Mass.
2003); Opinion of the Justices to the Senate, 802 N.E.2d 565 (Mass.
2004).

As must be apparent, given the remarkable persistence of the common law, its greatest strength lay in its adaptability. Deciding disputes without reference to a code, or originally in most cases even a statute, the judges almost necessarily resorted to reasoning from case to case by analogy. Practice in analogical reasoning is better preparation for dealing with the unexpected than explication of texts. While statutes may be more systematic and less tied to specific incidents (although this is far from universal), and while they are certainly capable of effecting drastic reform more speedily than law based on precedent,[52] they are also dependent on the uncertain attention of the legislature and its ability, both in general and to anticipate future developments. With its emphasis on courts, in the daily business of resolving disputes, the common law fostered an intensely practical frame of mind. "As between A and B, who has the better claim?" is a more focused and more easily answered question than "Who in all such cases has the best claim in all the world?"[53] Putting courts at the center inevitably made the judge rather than the legislator the hero of common-law history.

52. See Watson, *supra* note 27, at 182.

53. So in the early history of the common law the writ of right yielded to the possessory assizes. See Kenelm Edward Digby, An Introduction to the History of the Law of Real Property 108–111 (1897). For instances in which later courts lost their way, see John V. Orth, Russell v. Hill *(N.C. 1899): Misunderstood Lessons*, 73 N.C. L. Rev. 2031–2061 (1995); John V. Orth, *What's Wrong with the Law of Finders and How to Fix It*, 4 Green Bag 2D 391 (2001).

But the centrality of the judge in the common law is more than just historical fact. The antiquity of the common law meant that it predated not only statutes and constitutions but also all formal means of professional education. Common-law lawyers learned their law the medieval way: by apprenticeship, organized to one degree or another in a guild. (With law, of course, the reference is to the historic Inns of Court.) Necessarily, therefore, common-law judges were recruited from practice.[54] By the time modern law schools appeared in the nineteenth century, this pattern of recruitment was too well established to change—or even particularly to notice. Law schools simply picked up where apprenticeship left off and did not radically alter the nature of the judicial profession. Indeed, law schools (particularly American law schools, with their characteristic means of instruction from "casebooks") powerfully reinforced the traditional judicial role—in contrast to civil law systems with "career judiciaries," judges recruited on graduation, starting in the lowest courts and rising over time to higher and higher courts.[55]

Recruiting judges from among the ranks of successful lawyers inevitably introduced an element of dynamism into the common-law system. Not only was the common law

54. Professor Milsom emphasizes the technical complexity of common-law procedure: "Royal judges ceased altogether to be recruited from church and university and came to be chosen only from those who practiced in English courts.... [I]t was the practitioner's skill that the judge now needed." MILSOM, *supra* note 11, at 3–4.

55. *See* WATSON, *supra* note 27, at 176.

originally the product of creative judges, its continued vitality depended on judges, some of whom at least were willing to be more than mere passive participants. To the argument that he apply existing law even if unsatisfactory and then correct the result with legislation, Lord Mansfield once exclaimed, "What! pass a judgment to do mischief, and then bring in a bill to cure it?"[56] In the days before separation of powers à la Montesquieu, English judges were far less reluctant to legislate from the bench. In America, sanctioned by tradition and emboldened by custody of the constitution, judges are still active lawmakers.

The persistence of the common law is the story of adaptation, as might be expected. No human institution endures for eight centuries without change. In the process, it was so transformed that its medieval origins go largely unnoticed today. But the common law not only reacted to its environment, it also interacted with it. Statutes and constitutions in common-law systems are distinctively "common law," however odd it seems to think of a common-law statute or constitution. And modern law schools inculcate common-law methods, often without conscious recognition of the fact by

---

56. *Bishop of London v. Ffytche* (H.L. 1783), *reported in* T. CUNNINGHAM, THE LAW OF SIMONY 174 (1784). Mansfield's query was later quoted by Best, C. J., in *Fletcher v. Lord Sondes,* 3 Bing. 501, 580, 130 Eng. Rep. 606, 637 (H.L. 1826). In context, Lord Mansfield's outburst is perfectly understandable: the House of Lords combined its appellate role with legislative powers. *See generally* ROBERT STEVENS, LAW AND POLITICS: THE HOUSE OF LORDS AS A JUDICIAL BODY, 1800–1976 (1978).

either students or teachers. In a famous lecture a century ago, Maitland argued that in the late sixteenth century English law faced the threat of displacement by the revived Roman law, as happened across continental Europe, and famously attributed the common law's survival to its tradition of professional training. It was the occasion of his oft-quoted epigram "taught law is tough law."[57] Whether or not he was right about the threat—and Professor Thorne thought the thesis "completely mistaken"[58]—Maitland was certainly right to remind us of the power of priority, or inertia. The common law was there first, deeply rooted and functioning. It survived the Continental revival of Roman law. With some adjustments, it survived successive revolutions—economic, political, and social—and the advent of statutes and constitutions. It even survived the development of new forms of legal education. It is with us yet, omnipresent and therefore often unobserved.

57. F. W. Maitland, English Law and the Renaissance 18 (1901). The epigram is often misunderstood to refer to the harshness of classroom law, rather than to its durability.

58. S. E. Thorne, *English Law and the Renaissance, in* S. E. Thorne, Essays in English Legal History 187, 187 (1985).

5

The Ideology of the Common Law

In 1869, in his role as chairman of the Royal Commission on Trade Unions, Sir William Erle, former chief justice of the Court of Common Pleas, produced a memorandum on the law relating to labor organizations. In his introductory remarks he described individualism as the hallmark of the common law.[1] An employment contract was therefore conceptualized as an agreement between an individual employer and an individual worker, creating a relationship still referred to as master and servant.[2] The consequence of that concept was to make collective bargaining difficult and the legal status of trade unions precarious without statutory authority. A focus on the rights of individuals also affected the law

1. WILLIAM ERLE, THE LAW RELATING TO TRADE UNIONS passim (1869).

2. For a discussion of the changing terminology, see JOHN V. ORTH, COMBINATION AND CONSPIRACY: A LEGAL HISTORY OF TRADE UNIONISM, 1721–1906, at 144–145 (1991).

concerning strikes, limiting strikers to persuasion of individual workers not to keep working.[3]

In America a similar emphasis on the individual, this time located in the U.S. Constitution, specifically in the due process clauses of the Fifth and Fourteenth Amendments, led eventually to decisions such as *Lochner v. New York* in 1905, which found regulations concerning the hours of labor of adult males an unwarranted interference with the freedom of a worker who wanted to work longer hours.[4] The rise of "freedom of contract" and its ultimate demise form one of the most dramatic developments in twentieth-century constitutional history.[5] Although economic individualism in its constitutional form has largely vanished, the claim has been restated with respect to constitutional protection for privacy in individual decisions concerning intimate, specifically sexual, behavior.[6] In the economic arena, the argument for constitutional protection has been replaced with the claim that the rules of the common law governing private economic relations are suffused with individualism. The common law

---

3. *See id.* at 118–135.

4. 198 U.S. 45 (1905).

5. *See generally* THE STATE AND FREEDOM OF CONTRACT (Harry N. Scheiber ed. 1998).

6. *See* JOHN V. ORTH, DUE PROCESS: A BRIEF HISTORY 73–84 (2003). *See also Lawrence v. Texas,* 539 U.S. 558 (2003) (sodomy), reversing *Bowers v. Hardwick,* 478 U.S. 186 (1986); *Goodridge v. Department of Public Health,* 798 N.E.2d 941 (Mass. 2003) (same-sex marriage); Opinion of the Justices to the Senate, 802 N.E.2d 565 (Mass. 2004) (same).

is said to incorporate principles of economic efficiency.[7] The two claims—of an inherent individualism in the common law and of the common law's presumed economic rationality—are related, since classical economics focuses on individual choice.

But a moment's reflection raises questions about these claims. The U.S. Constitution and its amendments might (or might not) incorporate the economic ideas of the eighteenth and nineteenth centuries, but the common law was a product of the Middle Ages, having originated in England in the late twelfth century, and the medieval world was certainly precapitalist and (by definition) premodern. The individual was not at the center of medieval thought, nor were commercial transactions frequent enough to permit the development of sophisticated economic theories. Had the common law been secretly harboring modern ideas all along? Or had it been consciously reoriented?

On examination, it appears that the strongest claims concerning economic rationality are based on the rules concerning torts and contracts, but the truth is that for most of its long history the common law had few such rules. It was only in the late eighteenth century, and more particularly in the nineteenth century, that they began to be formulated. Treatises on the subjects first appeared at that time. John Joseph

7. *See, e.g.*, RICHARD A. POSNER, AN ECONOMIC ANALYSIS OF LAW 505 (3d ed. 1986); Paul Rubin, *Why Is the Common Law Efficient?* 6 J. LEGAL STUDIES 51 (1977).

Powell's essay, published in 1790, plausibly claimed to be the first English book on the law of contracts.[8] And in America, Joseph Story—Supreme Court justice, law school lecturer, and prolific author—candidly admitted that "the common law was an *utter stranger* to the principles of commercial jurisprudence." "Almost all the principles, that regulate our commercial concerns," he continued, "are of modern growth, and have been engrafted into the old stock of the law."[9] Yet apparently it never occurred to Story, who wrote on commercial topics from bailments to promissory notes, to write a treatise on contracts.[10] That was left to his son, the lawyer and artist William Wetmore Story, whose *Treatise on the Law of Contracts Not under Seal* first appeared in 1844, the year following his father's death. A revised and expanded second edition appeared three years later but was soon overshadowed by what was to become the standard text, Theophilus Parsons's two volumes on contracts, first published in 1853–1855. Treatises

8. JOHN JOSEPH POWELL, ESSAY UPON THE LAW OF CONTRACTS AND AGREEMENTS (1790).

9. Joseph Story, *Growth of the Commercial Law, in* MISCELLANEOUS WRITINGS OF JOSEPH STORY 269, 272 (William W. Story ed. 1852) (italics in original).

10. *See* GRANT GILMORE, THE DEATH OF CONTRACT 11 (1974). Story published commentaries on bailments (1832), the U.S. Constitution (3 vol. 1833), conflict of laws (1834), equity jurisprudence (2 vol. 1836), equity pleading (1838), agency (1839), partnership (1841), bills of exchange (1843), and promissory notes (1845). He was planning, so he told Charles Sumner before he died, further commentaries on shipping, insurance, equity practice, admiralty, the law of nations, and, finally, a book of reminiscences. 2 LIFE & LETTERS OF JOSEPH STORY 573–574 (William W. Story ed. 1851).

on tort law did not appear until the middle of the nineteenth century, the earliest not in England, the home of the common law, but in the commercial republic of the United States.[11]

This is not, of course, to say that issues concerning injuries and agreements did not arise in the first 600 years of common law history, although they were certainly not so common then as they are now, after the commercial and industrial revolutions have transformed society and economic relations. But the questions that did arise were resolved out of sight, in procedural operations and in the unexamined deliberations of juries. By contrast to the relatively late emergence of law books on contract and tort, Glanvill's Latin treatise on writs, the essence of medieval procedure, dates to the late twelfth century.[12] Early lawsuits settled disputes without settling questions of substantive law, so progress depended on procedural changes that would allow such questions to emerge.[13]

This emphasis (or overemphasis) on procedure may have suited the medieval mind, and it was morally acceptable because the rules were presumed to be accessible to all, drawn as they were from natural law, "written in their hearts."[14] On the eve of the American Revolution, the division of labor

11. Francis Hilliard, The Law of Torts (1859). *See* G. Edward White, Tort Law in America: An Intellectual History 4 (1985); S.F.C. Milsom, A Natural History of the Common Law 13 (2003).

12. Treatise on the Laws and Customs of the Realm of England Commonly Called Glanvill (G.D.G. Hall ed. 1993).

13. Milsom, *supra* note 11, at 2.

14. Romans 2:15 (KJV). *See also* Jer. 31:33 (KJV).

between judge and jury—the former to decide the law, the latter the facts—was not yet firmly established, and it was still standard practice to leave the decision of commercial cases to the jury, often without instructions.[15] A general verdict certainly resolved the dispute but gave no indication of the reason for the decision and set no precedent.[16]

As confidence in the intelligibility of natural law declined and the complexity of economic and social arrangements increased, exposition of the rules became ever more necessary. Contract rights were becoming as valuable as land, and rules to facilitate planning were becoming as necessary for merchants as they had long been for landowners. But it was not until the reform of legal procedure begun by Lord Mansfield, chief justice of the Court of King's Bench in the last half of the eighteenth century, that the legal issues were brought into the open.[17] Since the rules of procedure were within the

15. For the experience of one state, see JOHN PHILLIP REID, CONTROLLING THE LAW: LEGAL POLITICS IN EARLY NATIONAL NEW HAMPSHIRE (2004).

16. 12 WILLIAM HOLDSWORTH, HISTORY OF ENGLISH LAW 495 (1938).

17. *Id.* at 493–510. There may have been a motive other than simple traditionalism that had maintained the common-law practice. In the sixteenth century, Sir Thomas More is reported as complaining to his son-in-law, William Roper, that the judges' fear of decisional power was the chief preserver of the jury system. The judges preferred the current system, More explained, because "they may by the verdict of the jury cast off all quarrels from themselves upon them [the jurymen], which they account their chief defence...." WILLIAM ROPER, A LIFE OF SIR THOMAS MORE (written post-1535; first published 1626). Mansfield was not so timid, but his forwardness did expose him to severe criticism. *See* Thomas Jefferson, Letter to

purview of the court, Mansfield was able, without the need for parliamentary legislation, to clear away some of the obstacles to the development—again by the court—of substantive rules of law.[18]

When substance did at last begin to emerge from the shadow of procedure, it is hardly surprising that it was shaped by the regnant political and economic ideas of the time. The emphasis on the identity of reason and law, and the central role accorded the judge in the formation of the common law meant that the judge-made rules of the eighteenth and nineteenth centuries reflected the "best thinking" of the time. Assumption of the risk and the fellow-servant rule, contributory negligence, the fault basis of tort, the privity requirement in contract—all were products of the age. All were later qualified or eliminated. In their guise as rules of the common law, tort and contract can look far older than in fact they are. As Joseph Story pointed out, the new rules were simply "engrafted into the old stock of the law."[19] The lawyers' skill in teasing out apparent precedents concealed the operation. In time—and a relatively short time, at that—they could resemble the growth of ages.

Philip Mazzei (Nov. 28, 1785), *reprinted in* 9 THE PAPERS OF THOMAS JEFFERSON 67, 71 (Julian P. Boyd ed. 1954); *see also* Letter XLI (Nov. 14, 1770) by the pseudonymous English critic Junius, *reprinted in* THE LETTERS OF JUNIUS 206, 209–210 (John Cannon ed. 1978).

18. HOLDSWORTH, *supra* note 16, at 493–494. Control over the rules of procedure is one of the "secret sources of judicial power." See Essay 2.

19. *See* note 9, *supra*.

To say that the rules of tort and contract were created by the courts starting in the late eighteenth century, and not reaching final form until the late nineteenth or early twentieth century, is not to say that the older common law lacked an ideology. But it is to say that rules of procedure rather than substance formed a large part of that ideology, surely one of the reasons for the common law's uncommon persistence. Common-law procedure began simply as a means to resolve disputes in an orderly way, however strange some medieval ideas of orderliness may look today. That procedure became obfuscated by technicalities was a product of the times, of the inevitable sclerosis of human institutions, and of the lack of an academic tradition of rational criticism of the law. Technicalities served the professional interests of the lawyers by making the law mysterious, the preserve only of those paid to thread its intricacies. To some judges such as Baron Parke in the Court of Exchequer, it became an end in itself: "His keenest delight, it was said, was to non-suit a plaintiff in an undefended cause for some inaccuracy of expression."[20] Of the hypertechnicality of common-law procedure, the most that can be said is that it left a positive residue of meticulous attention to detail.

Stripped of its complexities, legal procedure schooled society in proper ways of doing things. Some of the most important ideas incorporated in the common law come from procedure: "Never make final decisions on *ex parte* represen-

20. C.H.S. Fifoot, English Law and Its Background 154–155 (1932).

tations." "Always explain the reasons behind a judgment."[21] Especially is this true of criminal procedure: the right to advance notice of the charges, to confront witnesses, to be heard in one's own defense, to be represented by counsel, to be tried by an impartial judge and jury, and so forth. The Bill of Rights contains a fairly complete catalog. The felt need to spell them out is indicative of their slow emergence and apparent precariousness. But criminal procedure was a late product of the common law. Here, too, until relatively recently in its long history, all the questions that mattered were asked and answered out of public hearing in the jury room.[22]

If common-law rules did not necessarily incorporate modern ideas of individualism, common-law procedure did at least assume that all parties in its courts were persons—in the case of corporations "fictitious persons"—with the consequence that slavery was unknown to the common law of England, whatever the case in other parts of the far-flung British Empire.[23] In a perverse way even jurists in American slave states

21. *See* John V. Orth, *Thinking about Law Historically, Why Bother?* 70 N.C. L. Rev. 287, 289 (1991).

22. Milsom, *supra* note 11, at 8.

23. Sommersetts Case, 20 Howell's State Trials 1 (1772). For a qualification, see Ruth Paley, *After* Somerset: *Mansfield, Slavery, and the Law in England, in* Law, Crime and English Society, 1660–1830, at 165 (Norma Landau ed. 2002). It is certainly true that a married woman's legal personality was submerged in her husband's during marriage, leading to invidious comparisons with slavery. *See, e.g.,* Sarah Grimke, *Legal Disabilities of Women, from* Letters on the Equality of the Sexes and the Condition of Women, *reprinted in* Freedom, Feminism, and the State 121 (Wendy McElroy ed. 1982).

acknowledged the fact by recognizing that slavery was essentially a lawless system, one that the common law, with its ingrained recognition of legal personality, could not easily accommodate. Justice Thomas Ruffin of North Carolina summed up his court's holding that a slaveholder could not be prosecuted for a criminal assault on a slave, even if cruel and excessive, with the chilling observation: "The power of the master must be absolute, to render the submission of the slave perfect."[24] Absolute power and perfect submission are, of course, inconsistent with the common law.

If tort and contract are relatively young, one area of the common law was surely old: property law. The earliest statutes in the English law book were concerned with it: De Donis Conditionalibus (1285),[25] the root of the fee tail, and Quia Emptores (1290),[26] the basis for free alienation of land. The oldest treatise on English property law was Littleton's *Tenures* from about 1481, so old in fact that it was written in French, the language of English lawyers for centuries after the Norman Conquest—a book that held its place in the canon, thanks to Sir Edward Coke's elaborate commentaries, until modern times. Land was livelihood, and a person's relationship to land determined social status as well as income.

24. *State v. Mann*, 13 N.C. 263 (1829).

25. 13 Edw. I, c. 1 (1285). The statute De Donis was enacted to overturn a line of common-law decisions, the source of the fee simple conditional. For its background and subsequent history, see John V. Orth, *Does the Fee Tail Exist in North Carolina?* 23 WAKE FOREST L. REV. 767, 773–778 (1988).

26. 18 Edw. I (1290).

What is more, because contract law was so undeveloped, land law was made to do extra duty, organizing labor and providing for family members.[27] Even in the law of property, it was only the law of real property, land law, that was truly primordial. A primitive law of personal property was tolerated until modern times because of the relative insignificance of things other than land. So uncomfortable was the common law with executory contracts that contracts for the sale of land—the most important type at the time—were turned into equitable titles by the doctrine of equitable conversion. To the bafflement of many lawyers (and their clients), rules on succession at death long differed depending on the type of property involved; in some states they still do.[28]

Land law did not particularly incorporate individualist or rational economic assumptions. Individual ownership was recognized but was not the paradigm it was to become. Although Blackstone asserted a presumption that all estates were held in sole ownership unless expressly declared to be otherwise,[29] the reality was that in Blackstone's day most English acres, certainly the most productive, were tied up in elaborate settlements, limiting the power of any one individual to dispose of or even to encumber the property. An estate in fee simple absolute held by one sole individual was very

27. *See* MILSOM, *supra* note 11, at 53; 2 HOLDSWORTH, *supra* note 16, at 355.

28. *E.g.,* N.C. Gen. Stat. § 29-14 (intestate share of spouse dependent on characterization of property as real or personal).

29. 2 WILLIAM BLACKSTONE, COMMENTEARIES ON THE LAWS OF ENGLAND 179 (1766).

rare. Ancient law, as Sir Henry Maine was astute to point out, "knows next to nothing of individuals. ... It is more than likely that joint-ownership, and not separate ownership, is the really archaic institution."[30] And Blackstone baffled even his contemporaries when he presented the traditional view that joint ownership of land by husband and wife as tenants by the entirety was not a form of co-ownership at all but a specialized form of sole ownership, the two being treated in law as one person.[31] The attempt to reconcile its common-law original and modern concepts of individual ownership still vexes the law of states that continue to recognize tenancies by the entirety.[32]

In practice, the units that owned land in medieval England were families—the royal family, aristocratic families, and the families of the gentry—as well, of course, as the church. Individual intention—of the essence in contract and, to a lesser extent, in tort—was not of paramount importance in property law, generally more involved with acquiring, preserving, and transmitting patrimonial land. "Giving effect to intentions" was not, as Professor Atiyah has reminded us, "the primary objective of the social order or of the law."[33] A characteristic that still distinguishes contract from property is the

30. HENRY MAINE, ANCIENT LAW 152–153 (1861).

31. *See* John V. Orth, *Tenancy by the Entirety: The Strange Career of the Common Law Marital Estate,* 1997 B.Y.U. L. REV. 35, 38–39.

32. *See* John V. Orth, *Tenancy by the Entirety, in* 4 THOMPSON ON REAL PROPERTY § 33.05, pp. 125–126 (2d Thomas ed. 2004).

33. P. S. ATIYAH, THE RISE AND FALL OF FREEDOM OF CONTRACT 122 (1979).

freedom it allows to design one's own legal relationship, to legislate as it were for the contracting parties. Contract law is flexible, while property law is meant to be predictable: choose from a catalog and follow the instructions, and you will get a standardized product.[34] The distinction may be justified on utilitarian grounds, but the origin is historical. Only in the comparatively recent past has property law been increasingly reconceptualized—and then only incompletely—as individual rather than patrimonial.[35]

The common law of property was riddled with rules that defeated intention, sometimes as with the Rule against Perpetuities intentionally so—one reason the venerable Rule seems to face certain extinction in the twenty-first century.[36] In other cases, rigid rules meant that you got what you wanted only if you (or your lawyer) knew the right words. For example, Blackstone instructed his students that "the word, heirs, is necessary in the grant or donation in order to make a fee, or inheritance." In consequence—until altered in modern times by statutes giving effect to intention—"if land be given to a man for ever, or to him and his assigns for ever, this vests

---

34. Thomas W. Merrill & Henry E. Smith, *Optimal Standardization in the Law of Property: The Numerus Clausus Principle*, 110 YALE L. J. 1, 3 (2000).

35. *See* John V. Orth, *Intention in the Law of Property: The Law of Unintended Consequences*, 8 GREEN BAG 2D 59 (2004).

36. *See* John V. Orth, *The Race to the Bottom in the Law of Property*, 9 GREEN BAG 2D 47 (2005).

in him but an estate for life,"[37] regardless of what was meant or even said in plain English. The common law's emphasis on procedure and property meant an insistence on form qualified by substantive rules concerning an individual's relation to land, particularly income-producing land. The effect was to do as much justice as was consistent with strict adherence to the rules. Planning was facilitated and judicial discretion cabined.

For most of the long history of the common law, property was its conceptual center. The displacement of property by contract occurred only in the nineteenth century.[38] The accumulating case law pointed the way; the emergence of an academic legal tradition sealed its fate. More than coincidence was at work when the law school dean who transformed American legal education, C. C. Langdell at the Harvard Law School, taught contract law. As a law student, he had assisted Professor Parsons in preparing his treatise; as a professor himself, he produced the first modern casebook, *Langdell on Contracts* (1871),[39] the model for all that followed. The second edition in 1880 was greeted by Oliver Wendell Holmes as the work of "the greatest living legal theologian."[40]

---

37. 2 WILLIAM BLACKSTONE, *supra* note 29, at 107 (citing Littleton's *Tenures* § 1). The same rule long prevailed in America. *See* 4 JAMES KENT, COMMENTARIES ON AMERICAN LAW 6 (12th ed. by O. W. Holmes 1873).

38. John V. Orth, *Contract and the Common Law, in* THE State AND FREEDOM OF CONTRACT 44–65 (Harry N. Scheiber ed. 1998).

39. 5 DICTIONARY OF AMERICAN BIOGRAPHY 585 (1932).

40. Book review, 14 AM. L. REV. 233 (1880).

The emergence of contract has certainly focused attention on individual volition, and increasing commercialization has brought economic analysis into the common-law tradition. Property rights are frequently described (in language more suitable to contract) as "investment-backed expectations,"[41] and an emphasis on intention has undercut traditional rules concerning transfer by deed or devise.[42] But the roots of economic individualism in the common law are far shallower than sometimes appears. Property and procedure are perennial concerns of any legal system, but they were uniquely at the heart of the common law. For centuries, the common law was concerned with little else. Any ideology, other than the ideology of procedure and property, is of comparatively recent growth, grafted into the old stock and periodically pruned.

41. See, e.g., *Penn Central Transp. Co. v. City of New York,* 438 U.S. 104, 127 (1978); *Hodel v. Irving,* 481 U.S. 704, 715 (1987).
42. See Orth, *supra* note 35, at 59–66.

Conclusion:

Looking Backward, Looking Forward

To judge rightly of the present we must oppose it to the past for all judgment is comparative, and of the future nothing can be known.

DR. JOHNSON, *Rasselas* (1759)

One of the great detective stories of antiquity is the story of Susanna and the elders from the Book of Daniel. Susanna was a pious Jewish woman living with her husband in Babylon. One hot day she decided to bathe in her private garden and ordered her maids to depart and lock the gates. While they were gone, two lecherous old men who had hidden in the garden to spy on her sprang forth and demanded sex. "If you refuse," they said, "we will testify against you that a young man was with you, and this was why you sent your maids away."[1] Susanna spurned them, and the elders raised

1. Susanna 21 (RSV), *in* THE OXFORD ANNOTATED APOCRYPHA (Bruce M. Metzger ed. 1977). The so-called Apocrypha is a collection of biblical

the hue and cry. At her trial Susanna was about to be con-
demned on the testimony of the two witnesses[2] when Daniel,
inspired by God, stepped forward and demanded that the
men be examined separately. "Under what tree did you see
them being intimate with each other?" he asked each in turn,
and got different answers.[3] Upon hearing this, "all the assembly shouted loudly and blessed God, who saves those who
hope in him." The elders were executed and Susanna freed.[4]

The story is a perennial favorite. Artists particularly liked
it because it gave biblical authority for the portrayal of femi-
nine charms.[5] It may also be taken as the paradigm of a cer-

---

literature that was included in the ancient Greek version of the Bible
known as the Septuagint and translated into Latin in the edition commonly known as the Vulgate. It is included in the canon recognized by
the Roman Catholic Church. Although translated into classic English in
the King James Version of the Bible in 1611, it is not nowadays included in
Bibles used by Protestant churches. The story of Susanna and the elders
appears in Catholic Bibles in Dan. 13.

2. Jewish law required two witnesses for conviction. Deut. 19: 15. The
common law had no such requirement, and in England statutes required
two witnesses only for treason, a requirement continued in the U.S. Constitution. U.S. CONST. art. III, § 3. For an episode in the history of labor
law involving a requirement of two witnesses, see JOHN V. ORTH, COM-
BINATION AND CONSPIRACY: A LEGAL HISTORY OF TRADE UNIONISM,
1721–1906, at 80–81 (1991).

3. Susanna 54–58.

4. Id. 60–62.

5. See GASTON DUCHET-SUCHAUX & MICHEL PASTOUREAU, THE BI-
BLE AND THE SAINTS 318–319 (1994) (an iconographic guide). A particu-
larly fine example by Tintoretto is in the Kunsthistorisches Museum in
Vienna.

tain type of legal narrative. The account begins with what actually happened, then moves ahead to the trial, which is treated as a search for what the reader already knows to be the truth. Will the legal system get it right? Suspense builds as events seem to conspire against the innocent. In this type of story, there is usually a happy ending: at the final moment, an ingenious detective steps forward and averts catastrophe by somehow demonstrating what really happened. In more sophisticated novels, such as Richard Wright's *Native Son* (1940), the verdict is accurate in legal terms—Bigger Thomas really is guilty as charged—but the reader is invited to condemn the racist society that conditioned his act.

This is one sense of "looking backward," knowing what happened and hoping, sometimes in vain, that others will see it too. Trials in the real world, of course, are not like this. The story always begins in medias res. There is no certainty about what went on in the past, or whether the truth will ever be known. An inquiry is undertaken, but the essential question is not about the past but about what to do next: in a civil trial, who wins? in a criminal trial, should the defendant be punished? What happened is almost always contested, the decision only a matter of belief—by a preponderance of the evidence in civil cases, beyond reasonable doubt in criminal trials. Because the consequences are so serious, particularly in criminal matters, the law limits the evidence that can be presented and its manner of presentation; inferences allowable (indeed indispensable) in ordinary historical research are sometimes forbidden.[6] It may seem surprising at first, but a trial is really not about looking backward, but about looking forward. The past is of concern only as it bears on the decision about what judgment to render in the present. Although many legal stories get to the trial looking backward, some describe the reality of legal life. An excellent example is James Gould Cozzens's novel *The Just and the Unjust* (1942), in which the murkiness of the past is not dispelled by divine intervention or an omniscient narrator.

The common law was made by practical lawyers who were interested in resolving disputes. Rules were relevant only to the extent they aided the process of moving forward. If a controversy could be settled without making or applying a rule, so much the better, and many disputes were in fact resolved on what today we would call procedural technicalities or by the unexplained verdict of a jury. Rules could not be dispensed with altogether, particularly those concerning property, not so much because they helped resolve disputes from the past as because they helped avoid disputes in the future. Rules allow people (and their lawyers) to plan ahead. Planning is possible only if rules are reasonably well known and reliably enforced.

In the development of legal institutions there comes a time when rules accumulate to the point that the law can be seen as a system of rules and not merely as a procedure for the res-

6. For further reflections, see John V. Orth, *Doing Legal History*, 14 (n.s.) IRISH JURIST 114 (1979).

olution of disputes. Then the stare decisis effect of a decision
is added to its res judicata effect.[7] It is at this point that accurate records become indispensable. Then, too, system makers
disconnect from the day-to-day reality of dispute resolution
and think things out, not in terms of "as between A and B
who has the better claim," but "who in all the world has the
best claim of all." The result can be logical, even beautiful,
what the classically educated call *elegantia juris*. Roman law
reached that stage centuries ago, and the end product, the
Corpus Juris Civilis, prepared at the command of the em-
peror Justinian in the sixth century, survived and became the
foundation of the modern legal systems of Europe—with the
exception of England, where the common law had struck
root early and thrived.[8]

The efforts of the system builders have left their mark on
the common law, especially after the development of modern
legal education in the nineteenth century. The result is not
always so helpful as it might seem. The law concerning the
finding of lost property is an example. The dispute in the typical lost-and-found case is between two persons, each claim-
ing the right to keep what was found pending the return of
its owner. The way the modern American law of finding has
developed is to analyze the various means by which the item
got there. It might have been dropped unwittingly and left

7. For an explanation of these terms, see Essay 2.
8. *See* Alan Watson, *Roman Law and English Law: Two Patterns of Development,* 36 LOYOLA L. REV. 247 (1990).

behind ("lost"), or placed in its location and then forgotten ("mislaid"), or hidden and not retrieved ("treasure trove"). It might even have been intentionally discarded ("abandoned"). Who gets to keep the item in this view depends on which of the above best describes how it got to where it was found. The first one to pick it up and keep it wins if the property was lost or abandoned, but if it was mislaid, the owner of the place of finding wins. Buried treasure went to the government in England, to the finder in America.[9] The trial in such cases is an attempt to tell the story from the beginning. The problem is that in every such case, how the item arrived at its location is always unknown or, at best, disputed. If it could be known with certainty how the item got there, the identity of its owner would most likely also be known or knowable, and the litigation would be unnecessary.[10]

Only in fiction can one tell the story from the beginning, with occasional pauses to make sure everyone else sees it the same way. For practical purposes we look backward in order to move forward. The common law has displayed an extraordinary ability to solve practical problems without hazarding in advance a comprehensive system of rules. From the standpoint of a lawyer trained in the Roman law tradition, the

9. The law is examined in more detail in John V. Orth, *What's Wrong with the Law of Finders and How to Fix It,* 4 GREEN BAG 2D 391 (2001).

10. It is possible to imagine a case in which a reliable witness saw the property being lost, mislaid, or buried without thereby learning anything about the identity of the owner, but none of the reported cases involves this situation.

lawyer in common-law systems seems to operate "at a lower level of abstraction."[11]

Backward glances such as those attempted in these essays do not allow a general narrative of the history of the common law, but they do reveal a thing or two that may be relevant in determining where we go from here. The common law developed in a homogeneous society in which right-thinking persons, certainly well-educated lawyers, would usually be able to agree on how a dispute should be resolved. For this reason, the common law functioned for centuries with only twelve judges, evenly distributed among three courts. An even number of judges was just as likely as an odd one to arrive at regular conclusions. By an irony of history, just at the moment consensus on the rules began to deteriorate, good behavior tenure insulated the judges from political pressure. The institutional novelty of odd numbers of judges provided a means to break ties but did nothing to guarantee general acceptance of their decisions. In extreme cases the political branches moved to adjust the size of the courts and explored other means to influence the outcome. As the difficulty of removing judges increased, so scrutiny of the candidates for judicial office increased as well. The process of nominating and confirming judges seems destined to attract ever more political attention.

Without the aid of a code or even frequent statutes, the common law achieved uniformity of results by developing a

11. *See* E. ALLAN FARNSWORTH, AN INTRODUCTION TO THE LEGAL SYSTEM OF THE UNITED STATES 73 (3d ed. 1996).

tradition of law reports, produced at first for private profit by briefless barristers. In time eminent judges themselves participated: the great Sir Edward Coke in England, in America William Cranch among federal judges and François-Xavier Martin in Louisiana. In order to maintain itself in the new constitutional system of the United States, the American judiciary pioneered a new means of judicial expression, "the opinion of the court." Coupled with newly official reports, these opinions crowded out the arguments of counsel as sources of law and, in an increasingly positivist milieu, came to be regarded as a specialized type of legislation. As they jockeyed with the legislative and executive branches, the judges exploited to the full their institutional advantage, but an increasingly fractionated bench, staffed by judges determined to make their individual mark, undermines the public support on which courts ultimately depend.

Codes confine judicial discretion, and the advent of written constitutions, a form of constitutional code, might have threatened the common-law tradition. Instead, they only enhanced judicial power as the judges responded to the instruments in typical common-law fashion, taking over their interpretation and the application of the new rules and procedures. Judicial review joined statutory construction and analogical reasoning in the judicial toolbox. Meanwhile, the force of common-law tradition blinded the judges to the potential conflict with constitutionally mandated separation of powers as they made and unmade the common law, guided by ever-fructifying "reason." Judicial lawmaking exposes the judges to political risk and reduces the perception of the judiciary as the "least dangerous branch."

The common-law system, with its emphasis on institutions rather than rules, made the law flexible to an extent not possible in rule-based systems. Common-law institutions and ways of doing business proved easily adaptable to changing circumstances and allowed the rules to be adjusted as needed. Never dominated by a single ideology—other than that necessarily associated with proper procedure and the law of property—the common law rather easily survived the change of regimes, political as well as economic and social. But the courts stand constantly exposed to the capture of jurisprudence by narrow and time-bound ideologies.

The vistas of the past are long; there is no comparable view looking forward. As to the near future, we can expect the common-law system to continue resolving disputes. Courts and judges will remain the center of attention, and the common law will continue to interact with constitutions and statutes in complex ways. Legal systems are hard to displace, and the Anglo-American tradition has been particularly averse to radical change. As to the far future, the vision clouds. We may legitimately ask whether humanity will always need law—common, civil, or canon. Millennialists in every age imagine a world without law, or at least one without lawyers. Sir Thomas More, himself a great lawyer, pictured Utopia in just this way. But then he located it nowhere on the map.

The question whether we will always need law reminds me of the question whether we will always need art or music. On that the experts are divided. A great art historian conceded that "mankind may some day outgrow its need for art."[12] A great musician, on the contrary, believed that "as long as the human race survives, music will be essential."[13] On the arts, I tend to agree with the musician. Law, of course, is not like art or music—except to the extent it responds to perennial, if not perpetual, human needs. Law will certainly remain with us as long as we remain the violence-prone, greedy, disputatious creatures we have always been. Even could we transcend that legacy—whether it be from evolution or original sin—we will still need an orderly means to arrange our affairs and resolve our inevitable disagreements. Conclusions will differ. For myself, I must admit that I believe that we will need law so long as we are recognizably human: on the last voyage of Spaceship Earth, on its last transit around the sun, the last sound to be heard from its human passengers, I predict, will be quarrelling about who gets the best seats.

12. W. H. Janson, History of Art: A Survey of the Major Visual Arts from the Dawn of History to the Present Day 9 (1962).

13. Yehudi Menuhin & Curtis W. Davis, The Music of Man 1 (1979).

Table of Cases

Table of Statutes

Subject Index

www.ingramcontent.com/pod-product-compliance
Lightning Source LLC
Chambersburg PA
CBHW061255220326
41599CB00028B/5661